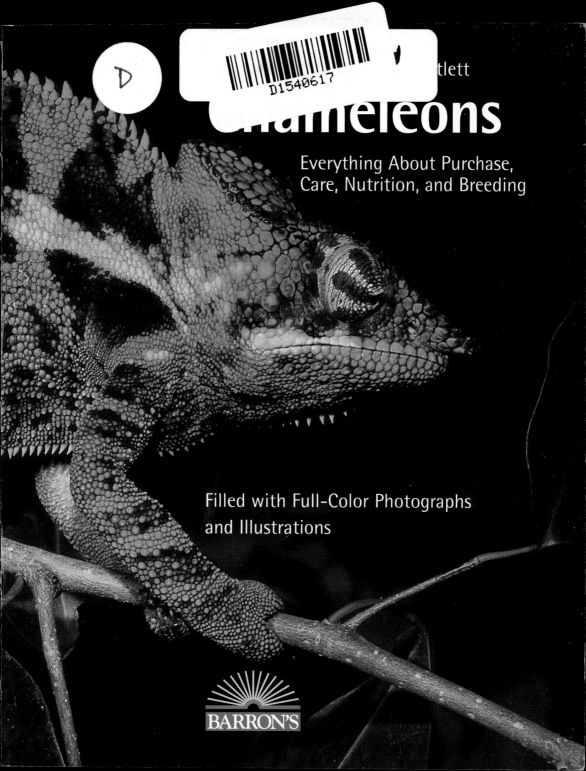

tlett

Chameleons

Everything About Purchase,
Care, Nutrition, and Breeding

Filled with Full-Color Photographs
and Illustrations

BARRON'S

CONTENTS

WHAT MAKES CHAMELEONS UNIQUE?

Chameleons are remarkable lizards with turreted eyes, extensible tongue, changeable color, prehensile tail, and bundled toes. They are among the most highly specialized and immediately recognizable of all reptiles.

All chameleons are initially of Old World distribution, but one or two species have escaped from captivity and can now be found in Hawaii, California, and Florida. Despite the frequency with which chameleons appear in the marketplace, as captives these solitary lizards require a dedicated regimen of daily care tailored to a particular species. Factors such as available humidity, cage temperature, and cage ventilation are now known to be of paramount importance.

Only a few species of chameleons are bred with any degree of regularity in captivity. Among those are the veiled, Jackson's, and panther chameleons. Most of the other available species are collected from the wild.

Females of the Mt. Meru Jackson's chameleon often bear a single horn.

Availability

When viewed on a species level, the availability of chameleons in the United States has been a revolving door. Those commonly seen at one time may become unavailable a few months later, then reappear in numbers several years hence. This has been most notable with the many Malagasy chameleons. More than 20 species of Malagasy origin were readily available in the 1990s, but only three are seen with any regularity today (2005). In the current marketplace the African chameleon species (including the tiny leaf chameleons) are most often found. But we hasten to add that several of those that are the most inexpensive and regularly available, the graceful chameleon, the Senegal chameleon, and the flap-necked chameleon among them, are also some of the most problematic captives.

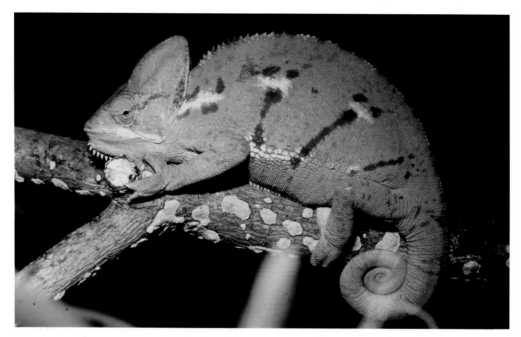

We urge that when you are considering a chameleon for a pet, you think past the initial monetary outlay and consider instead the facilities you can offer, and only then choose a species that will adapt well to your situation.

This adult female veiled chameleon never assumed breeding colors, and was entirely ignored by her male companion.

Color-Changing Ability

Although not all chameleons are capable of undergoing dramatic color changes, more than half of the 120-plus species readily do so. We have come to understand that, rather than being random, the color changes seen in chameleons have well-defined functions that are readily understood by the lizards themselves. Chameleons literally "speak with their skins."

The color changes are both physiological and physical. Stress (caused by territorial disputes with others of their own kind, adverse temperatures, injury, improper captive husbandry, or other factors) and activity induce chameleons to assume darker colors and more intricate, or at least better defined, patterns. Quiescent specimens experiencing optimum conditions are generally of paler coloration and display weaker patterns, or are patternless.

A particular color or pattern may indicate sexual receptivity or the opposite. Gravid female chameleons often assume and retain colors and/or patterns unlike those displayed at any other time in their lives. (When all factors pertaining to color and pattern change are considered, with more than 100 variations,

Bands may be prominent or almost absent on the two-striped chameleon.

it is the wide-ranging common chameleon, *Chamaeleo chamaeleon* of southern Europe and northern Africa that is the most variable.)

While on the subject of color, chameleons of the same species may be sexually dichromatic (differ in color by sex) and can vary in color by age and geographic origin as well. To illustrate the latter, at one part of its range an adult panther chameleon, *Furcifer pardalis*, may be an intense electric-turquoise in color, but a male from only a few hundred miles away may be orange and green banded. If the color of the chameleon species in which you are interested is of importance to you, be sure to ascertain the color of the example in question or, at least, of its parents.

Appearance

Collectively, chameleons have a laterally compressed body. Beyond that, many species are bizarrely adorned with casques, flaps, and horn-like nasal appendages on their heads.

Some also have sail-like vertebral crests on their backs and/or a caudal crest on the tail. A gular (throat) crest is also often present. Males are more generously adorned than females. A chameleon's toes are wrapped into opposing units, two on one side of each foot, three on the other. With tong-like action, the toes tightly grip the branches of trees and shrubs as the chameleon moves slowly about. The tails of the many arboreal species are very strongly prehensile.

Chameleons vary in size from the inch and a half (4 cm) overall length of the pygmy leaf chameleon of Madagascar to the more than 30 inches (80 cm) of the Oustalet's chameleon, also of Madagascar.

Reproduction Facts

Although most chameleons are egg-layers (oviparous), some (especially those from high altitudes) are live-bearers (ovoviviparous). Chameleons breed at early ages, have large numbers of eggs or young, and seem to have relatively short life spans in the wild.

Eyes

The eyes of a healthy chameleon are protuberant, turret-like, and the lids are fused except for a central aperture through which the pupil peers. Working independently of one another, one eye may be scanning the rear for an approaching enemy while the other watches the front or side.

When prey is sighted, the chameleon stalks slowly, haltingly forward, until it is about one body length away from the intended prey. Both eyes are then focused on the insect, thus creating binocular vision. Slowly the chameleon opens its mouth and shoots its tongue forward. In an instant the insect has been captured and the lizard is munching contentedly.

Tongue

The chameleon's tongue structure is unlike that of any other lizard. By the simultaneous contraction of numerous muscles, the tongue, often nearly as long as the body and head of the lizard, is projected quickly forward. The thickened tip has a central indentation as well as mucous-secreting glands. The prey insect is firmly grasped by and "glued" to the tongue tip of the chameleon. The tongue, insect secured, is then retracted. When fully retracted the tongue surrounds a portion of one of the hyoid bones. Once in the chameleon's strong jaws, the prey item is methodically and thoroughly masticated, then swallowed. So effective is this arrangement that larger species of chameleons have been known to successfully capture small rodents and birds.

The Chameleon Family

All chameleons belong to the family Chamaeleonidae, which is divided into two subfamilies. The "typical" and the dwarf chameleons are contained in the subfamily Chamaeleoninae, while the leaf chameleons are members of the subfamily Brookesiinae.

The genera contained in the subfamily Chamaeleoninae are *Chamaeleo, Bradypodion, Calumma,* and *Furcifer* (the genus *Chamaeleo* is divided into two subgenera: *Chamaeleo* and *Trioceros*). These, the typical and the dwarf chameleons, all move rather quickly, are more arboreal, are more capable of

All but invisible on a tree barely 3/4 inch (2 cm) in diameter, this adult male veiled chameleon is adept at keeping the tree between him and an approaching human.

Dwarfed by the lichens on which it is standing, Ramanantsoa's pygmy leaf chameleon is only about an inch and a half (3.8 cm) in overall length.

changing color, and have a proportionately longer, more prehensile tail than their predominantly terrestrial, leaf-like cousins. Males can be quite aggressive toward their own and closely related species.

The subfamily Brookesiinae contains only two genera of leaf chameleons, *Brookesia* and *Rhampholeon*. All leaf chameleons are diminutive and are also referred to as "stump-tailed chameleons." They are slow-moving, cryptic lizards that are characterized by their short, weakly prehensile tail, small size, and inability to undergo dramatic color changes. All have relatively benign dispositions.

A large and healthy Oustalet's chameleon traverses a limb.

Thermoregulation

Many chameleons are heliothermic (cold-blooded) creatures that thermoregulate. That is, they use the warmth of the sun and the coolness of the shade to attain and maintain the body temperature at which their body functions are the most efficient. That goal differs considerably by species. Species adapted to high elevations or other cooler climates are fully functional at considerably cooler body temperatures than a lowland rainforest species would be.

To quickly warm itself, a cold chameleon will flatten and tilt its body to best utilize the warming rays of the sun. When faster warming is desired, the creature darkens its color somewhat and lessens the volume of air contained in its lungs. Conversely, techniques used by a hot chameleon to reduce its body temperature include facing into the sun (thus presenting less body surface to absorb the warmth), moving into the shade, lightening its body color, and panting. Thus, not only is absorption of

TIP

A Word of Caution

Body temperatures that become either too hot or too cold can be debilitating or even fatal.

heat reduced, but panting causes moisture evaporation from the mucous membranes, which actually cools the lizard.

Brumation and Aestivation

Chameleons from high altitudes (or other areas that experience a significant drop in winter temperatures) brumate (hibernate), while those species from hot, seasonally dry regions may aestivate during periods of excessive warmth or drought. Both brumation and aestivation may last for a period of several weeks, during which the lizards remain burrowed beneath yielding substrates. However, some chameleon species found in areas that become cold but do not freeze may simply become quiescent while clinging to a branch.

Too Hot or Too Cold?

Be aware that many chameleons prefer coolness (not cold) over excessively warm conditions. To learn the temperatures at which your chameleons are most comfortable, read the species accounts contained in these pages. We have been unable to cover the needs of all 100-plus species of chameleons here, but, in many cases, it will be possible for you to

Male veiled chameleons glow like treetop beacons in the early morning sunshine.

extrapolate. Research both the range and the habitat of your species. If it is a montane form, opt for caging such as that shown for the little high-casqued chameleon or the big Jackson's chameleon. If it is a hot lowland form, provide the caging suggested for the veiled or the graceful chameleon.

Usumbara giant three-horned chameleons are pretty, alert, and reasonably hardy.

If you are totally unsure, opt toward cooler conditions but provide a warmed basking area. In other words, provide a thermal gradient. Allow the terrarium temperature to drop to between 65 and 68°F at night (18–20°C) and raise it to 72–78°F (22–26°C) in the daytime. The warmed basking area should enable the chameleon to elevate its body temperature to 86 to 90°F (29–33°C) if it chooses. Some species (especially gravid females) will avail themselves of the hot spot; others will not.

The Solitary Chameleon

Although in the wild a fair number of some chameleons may occasionally be found in a single tree, none of these creatures could be called truly communal. In the wild, *most* are either preferentially solitary or found in pairs.

If your cage is sufficiently large, most species of chameleons can be kept in pairs or trios of one male and two females. However, you must continually monitor the interactions of all members of the group and be aware of the effects of low-level stress. Even if not overt, the dominance factor can prevent subordinate specimens from feeding, drinking, or resting normally or sufficiently. Monitor your chameleons frequently. Chameleons that are compatible when not sexually mature or sexually active may become formidable adversaries when mature or in breeding condition. Agonistic behavior between adult males of the typical and dwarf chameleons is almost a certainty. Leaf chameleons are less territorial and can be kept communally in large terraria or cages.

"Family groups" of chameleons that have been compatible in large cages may no longer be so if changed to smaller quarters. Again, monitor your groups closely.

In the normal course of breeding activities, the males (the larger sex in most chameleon species) may seriously injure the female. Be ready to intervene and cage the animals separately if necessary.

ACQUIRING A CHAMELEON

As a group, chameleons are not very hardy, but some are more easily maintained than others. Because of the almost inherent difficulties in keeping many chameleons, it is best to start with a hardy species.

Select Healthy Specimens

It is very important that you choose a chameleon that is in obvious good health from a reputable and knowledgeable source. Unfortunately, many sellers of chameleons fail to comprehend the animals' complexities and true needs. This results in the lizards being maintained in suboptimal conditions. Find a supplier who can accurately answer your questions. To determine accuracy, compare some of the supplier's answers to your questions to the information contained in this book. They should jibe. If pet-shop employees cannot satisfactorily answer your questions, the chances are excellent that they are not caring for their chameleons properly.

If you visit a shop that houses its adult male chameleons several to a cage or crowded into a cage with other lizard species, the store's husbandry techniques are flawed and other information may also be. Shop elsewhere.

Pick Captive-Bred

Captive-bred or well-acclimated wild-collected chameleons may be more expensive than fresh imports, but purchasing the former will help assure your success.

Insects consumed by chameleons often harbor parasites that are, in turn, passed on to the lizards. However, since well-acclimated and captive-bred chameleons are less stressed than fresh imports, the endoparasites they harbor are less likely to proliferate to pathogenic proportions. Additionally, the purchase of captive-bred/captive-hatched chameleons is a valid conservation tool, reducing the draw on wild chameleon populations.

Prepare the caging for your chameleon in advance. The chances are excellent that you will be purchasing a (somewhat) stressed lizard. There must be a secure cage in which it can feel safe upon its arrival.

Unlike her male counterpart, this female Werner's chameleon has only a single horn.

Two-striped chameleons are a small live-bearing species.

Keeping Your Chameleon

To maintain them successfully, and especially to breed them, chameleons (like all reptiles) require that certain basic husbandry techniques be followed. Among these criteria are

✔ thermoregulation
✔ dietary and drinking considerations
✔ cage setup

Because of their inherent differences (including habitat preference), certain chameleon species are more easily kept in very humid regions, while others may be more comfortable in areas having a low humidity. Some chameleons will prefer cool, temperate regions, and others will do best in the subtropics.

For example, montane (mountain-dwelling) species thrive in areas where summers are cool and winters are relatively benign. Chameleons from tropical Africa and Madagascar may do fine in the summer in subtropical regions, but they will require winter heating. Research the needs of the lizards and institute the needed regimen of husbandry.

TIP

For the Novice

We feel that the veiled chameleon, *Chamaeleo c. calyptratus*, is the best choice for beginners. If *any* chameleon could be dubbed hardy, the term would be best applied to the veiled chameleon, which is large, pretty, and, unlike most other chameleons, omnivorous (another plus in husbandry).

═══ TIP ═══

Debilitating Stressors

Chameleons respond very unfavorably and very rapidly to various stresses. They are quickly debilitated by any degree of
- ✔ dehydration
- ✔ food shortages
- ✔ vitamin imbalances

The Usumbara leaf chameleon is a slow-moving leaf mimic that plays dead when startled.

Oustalet's chameleon is similar in appearance to the spiny chameleon but has smaller scales and more of them in the vertebral crest.

CHECKLIST

The Selection Process

Even the easiest to keep of the true chameleons are difficult in comparison with many other lizard species. Because of this it is very important that you start with a healthy animal. Here's what to look for:

1. Purchase captive-born or captive-hatched chameleons whenever possible.

2. If no captive-produced chameleon is available, accept only well-acclimated animals.

3. Many importers now routinely test and treat freshly imported chameleons for internal parasites. Try to ascertain that this has been done.

4. The chameleon you choose must have good body weight. Do not purchase one that has the ribs, shoulder, or pelvic girdles strongly evident.

5. The lizard must appear alert.

6. The pupil opening must be round with no encrustations on the lids. The eyes should be protuberant, not sunken.

7. The lizard should not have any swellings on toes, legs, tail, or body.

8. The specimen should not be gasping or breathing with opened mouth.

9. There should be no swellings, redness, or scabs on the lips.

10. Many chameleons have subcutaneous parasites. These are visible as raised welts. Do not purchase a chameleon on which these are visible.

11. Try to choose chameleons that have been housed individually.

12. Select a reptile-certified veterinarian who will be available if necessary.

At one week of age, veiled chameleons show no contrasting colors.

Smaller in size and having smaller rostral appendages, Fischer's chameleon is less favored by hobbyists.

Because of the very different lifestyles embraced by the various chameleons, it is difficult to generalize regarding these lizards. For particulars we urge that you read the various species accounts in this book. In each we have discussed the needs, as far as are currently known, of several individual species, and in each we have tried to mention individual peculiarities.

Here we will mention a few standardized mannerisms and needs of the chameleons as a group.

✔ Although most female chameleons will rather peacefully coexist with others of their own species and sex, sexually mature males of the same (or closely allied) species will fight savagely with other males. When housed in mixed-sex groups (one male and one female or one male and two females), sexually mature chameleons of all species should be provided with numerous visual barriers (branches, tree limbs, etc.) in their cage. Visual barriers may

Chameleons with inflatable gular areas use them to signify territoriality.

even be necessary between cages.

✔ Agonism (antagonism, unease) between male chameleons will be manifested by rapid color changes, lateral flattening of the body, head bobbing, mouth gaping, pursuit, and actual skirmishing. Males of closely allied species will fight as persistently as males of the same species. Head bobbing and nodding and color changes may also indicate courtship when used by a male in the presence of a female.

Pincer-like toes provide a strong grip for arboreal species.

✔ Stylized stalking, intent staring, and halting movements indicate an interest in a prey item (when employed by a hungry, hunting chameleon).

✔ Of the two chameleon groups, the members of the terrestrial short-tailed chameleon group (genera *Brookesia* and *Rhampholeon*) seem to resent handling less than most of the arboreal species. However, no chameleon likes to be handled. As a generality, chameleons should be considered display lizards that should not be handled.

✔ Although the vast majority of chameleons are tropical, many dwell in the comparative coolness of mountain elevations. Most chameleons

Now you see it, now you don't: the chameleon using its tongue to catch an insect.

YOUR CHAMELEONS

prefer temperatures between 68 and 82°F (17–28°C). Terraria should provide thermal gradients. A hot spot of 88–92°F (30–34°C) may be used by some species if it is provided. Nighttime temperatures can be allowed to drop by a few additional degrees.

✔ While terrestrial chameleons will often lap water from a dish (especially if roiled by an aquarium air stone) or lap droplets from freshly misted substrate, arboreal species often insist on drinking pendulous droplets from leaves and limbs while in elevated positions.

✔ Most chameleons are primarily insectivorous. Some of the larger species may accept newly born mice in their diets, but these should be fed sparingly. Virtually all insist that the prey be alive and moving. Some chameleon species also consume a fair amount of foliage and blossoms. Do not ignore this aspect of their diets.

✔ Cages for arboreal chameleon species should be vertically oriented; those for terrestrial species should be horizontally oriented. Although the comparatively few desert chameleon species prefer low humidity in the cage, most chameleons enjoy high relative humidity but well-ventilated conditions.

Tails, whether prehensile or not, are important balancing tools for chameleons.

✔ As they grow, chameleons shed their skin periodically. Shedding occurs more frequently when the lizard is growing rapidly. The skin is most usually shed in "patchwork" fashion. The entire skin, including the eyelids and toes, is shed.

✔ The tails of arboreal species are prehensile and are often held coiled like a watch spring when the animals are at rest. The tails of terrestrial species are less prehensile and do not tightly coil.

✔ The condition of an ill or injured chameleon can deteriorate quickly. Observe your pets carefully and seek medical assistance when necessary.

HOUSING

The type of housing you provide for a chameleon depends on several factors—including the type of chameleon you own, the number you plan to house together, if at all, and where you live.

The temperatures at which chameleons are comfortable—and the temperatures you will need to offer in your caging—vary according to species. Desert/dry savanna species, such as the veiled or the North African subspecies of the common chameleon, prefer warmer temperatures but lower humidity than montane forest species such as the Jackson's or Elliot's chameleons. The desert forms are even able to withstand temperatures as high as 95°F (35°C) with no ill effects. High-altitude species would be quickly and noticeably distressed by such warmth.

Nighttime temperatures can be (in fact, should be) somewhat cooler than daytime highs for all chameleons.

Provide a warmed basking area (surface temperature of 88°F [31°C]) during the daylight hours by prudent use of a floodlight. Except in the case of the few terrestrial chameleon species that will bask on the ground, the warmed basking area should be an elevated

The Uluguru mountain leaf chameleon is a tiny, stump-tailed leaf-mimic.

climbing branch slender enough to be easily grasped by the chameleon.

Caging Types

Wood and Wire

Enclosure size: Chameleons should be provided with the largest possible enclosures. Those that we use most frequently measure 48 × 30 × 71 inches (121 × 76 × 180 cm) overall. All are on large casters (wheels) to facilitate easy moving. The uprights of the frames and the door assembly are made from untreated 2×2s. The top and bottom are solid pieces of marine plywood. The top has had the center removed, leaving a rim about 6 inches (15 cm) wide all the way around. The sides, front, back, door, and top are covered with 1/8-inch (0.3-cm) mesh hardware cloth that is stapled tightly in place. The 30-inch (76-cm) width and the 71-inch (180-cm) height (which includes the casters) allow these cages to be easily wheeled through average interior and exterior doorways. Thus, it is a simple matter to wheel the

Temperature Perfect

A cage that is maintained in the low 70s by day and in the low 60s by night (21–23°C days, 16–18°C nights) will prove ideal for many chameleon species.

cages outside, to allow the chameleons to partake of natural sunlight and rain. The cage furniture consists of a full-height ficus tree (usually *F. benjamina*) and a number of dead-limb perches of suitable diameter.

Cool weather: Because we are located in temperate Florida, we can keep our chameleons outside for most of the year. If left outdoors during cool weather, the cages are wrapped in clear 4-mil plastic sheeting. This is stapled firmly in place on three sides. The cage front (the door side) is covered by a separate piece of plastic sheeting that is stapled only at the top and is weighted at the bottom. This can be rolled up and out of the way on warm days. A heat lamp is activated when necessary. Except for the removable front and top, the vinyl can (and probably should) remain in place throughout the winter months to assure the comfort of the lizards. During cool weather, chameleons will spend hours basking in the sunshine. The cage bottom can be left bare, or a low frame can be installed that will retain a clean sand substrate. (Although we do use sand on the bottoms of our cages, we merely pile it high in the cage center and let it seek its own level. Occasionally it gets washed from the cage during storms and is then replaced.)

Smaller cages: While the large (step-in) cages described above are our preference, especially for such large species as veiled, Oustalet's, Parson's, and Meller's chameleons, we have used smaller cages equally well for both large and small species. We have successfully kept small chameleon species such as carpets, high-casqued, Elliot's, and others of similar size in wood and wire cages that measured 24 × 18 × 36 inches (60 × 45 × 90 cm). A potted shrub of some type and horizontal limbs for perching are always incorporated into the decor. Obviously, these smaller cages can easily be carried outside in warm weather and inside in cooler weather.

Ground dwellers: For forest-floor chameleons, such as the interesting little leaf chameleons (genera *Brookesia* and *Rhampholeon*), and for the common chameleon (the most terrestrial member of the genus *Chamaeleo*), the cage height can be lessened somewhat. For these species a height of 12 to 18 inches (30–45 cm) will suffice.

We use caging of wood and wire construction, as chameleons prefer well-ventilated quarters with no standing moisture. It is easier to create such a habitat with wood and wire cages than it is with glass terraria. The use of 1/8-inch mesh in the cage construction will keep all but the smallest food insects from escaping. Although this mesh size is smaller than many hobbyists use, our chameleons have never had any broken toes or toenail trauma.

Some researchers recommend that only plastic-coated wire be used, to avoid abrasion of snout or foot damage. Whichever type you choose, it is important to use only wire with a smooth surfaced.

Baby chameleons of all species, or one or two adults of most small species, can be housed in a cage having a diameter of 18 inches (45 cm) and a height of 2 feet (60 cm).

The Value of Shrubs

An isolated shrub can serve admirably as a chameleon home during suitable weather. We have a pair of Usumbara giant three-horned chameleons, *Chamaeleo deremensis*, residing in a crepe myrtle with a spreading top about 12 feet (3.5 m) in diameter. The crepe myrtle seems perfect for these lizards. The shrub grows in an area of the yard that is bathed by midday sunlight. Its small leaves allow the sunlight to penetrate deeply into the interior. The branches are of small diameter and are easily grasped by the pincer-like feet of the chameleons. The flower heads of the shrub draw numbers of insects on which the lizards can dine. And the crown of the bush is large enough for the lizards to stay out of each other's sight if they choose (and they often do choose this path of avoidance).

Of course, keeping a pair of coveted lizards in an open shrub can have almost as many drawbacks as benefits. The chameleons are vulnerable to attack from predators (we have many hawks, crows, opossums, and raccoons in the neighborhood), or the lizards could drop from the shrub and escape. They could even ingest a toxic insect of some sort.

If you do choose to use a shrub, you can easily make it more escape- and predator-proof. Since chameleons are more apt to climb down a trunk than to drop from the limbs, design a ring of aluminum flashing 18 inches (45 cm) high that encircles the trunk but that is about 3 feet (90 cm) distant from it on all sides. This will prevent casual escape by the lizards. Predators can be deterred by draping bird netting (designed to keep birds away from crops and fruit-bearing trees) loosely over the shrub. This netting usually has mesh that is too small for a large chameleon to escape through.

Crepe myrtle is a "busy" bush and has many small branches into which we can wedge a plastic container (with drain holes on the bottom) holding a few vitamin-enhanced crickets, which should be replaced daily. The entire shrub is sprayed gently with a garden hose every day or two. Then the chameleons drink the pendulous droplets from the leaves. The lizards avail themselves of the natural sunlight, basking on an exposed branch when the weather is cool and striding into the cool shade when the temperature is hotter than they prefer.

The lizards' body color indicates that they are content in this setting, and their rounded bellies and protruding eyes show that they are getting ample food and moisture.

We are able to use this shrub for most of the year, but even in colder climates a similar setup can be used during the hot days of summer.

Aquariums

There are times and places when decor and/or space constraints make wood and wire cages impractical. For those times and places there are hosts of commercially constructed or homemade aquariums that double admirably as terrariums.

Horizontal or vertical: When figuring just how you're going to adapt your aquarium tank, always consider the proposed residents. For arboreal chameleons, the height of the terrarium deserves as much consideration as the floor space. If you are housing terrestrial chameleons, then, of course, the height of the cage is far less important.

Basic layout: The glass terraria may be oriented in the standard horizontal ("top up") position for terrestrial chameleon species or placed in an upright, vertical position for arboreal species. A suitable top (or front, as the case may be) will need to be provided. With the

A large, wood and wire cage, containing shrubs and other visual barriers, will adequately house a pair of large chameleons.

standard orientation this poses no problem. However, when the upright orientation is preferred, formulating an escape-proof front becomes more difficult. This may be approached from two angles. First, if not too heavy, a glass front may be cut and held in position with a hinge of silastic aquarium sealant. A hook and hasp may be similarly held in place on the opposite side. We have found that if the edge of the glass door rests flush against the table or stand top (or the inside glass of the aquarium), the sealant hinge is much less stressed. The second method is to sit your terrarium an inch or two (2.5–5 cm) off the flat surface on blocks or legs. A tightly fitting framed front can then simply be slipped over the open side.

Habitats

Two basic habitats may be replicated in caging. Each habitat can have both terrestrial and arboreal applications.

Savanna Terrarium

Savannas are areas of transition between or at the edge of forest, woodland, or desert. The treed and sunlit edges of these spacious, rolling, otherwise sparsely vegetated glades are the habitats of many chameleon species. Different soil formation and moderated rainfall provide a habitat much different from that of either surrounding desert or woodland/forest. Savannas often host various species of moderately, or at least seasonally, lush grasses, as well as thornscrub and other formidably armed trees. Areas of rocky scree may be present. A dry savanna will work well for the desert chameleon species.

Savannas are often subjected to weather extremes in the form of temperature, rainfall, or other such climatic vagaries. The plant community found in savannas is difficult to maintain in terraria over extended periods. Periodic refurbishing of your terrarium vegetation will most likely be necessary.

The basics: A thick layer of sandy humus into which a liberal helping of variably sized rocks has been mixed should comprise the substrate of the savanna terrarium. Seedling acacias and clumped grasses, as well as weathered branches, cactus skeletons, and strategically placed rocks and rock formations, can be used for decorative purposes. The savanna terrarium plant community will require somewhat more water than that in the desert terrarium. However, even with judicious care, many plants (especially the grasses) will need replacing each season. The plants can be either potted or planted directly into the terrarium substrate. We prefer the latter, simply for aesthetics. A screen top will assist you in keeping the lower humidity preferred by most savanna-dwelling chameleon species.

Woodland/Forest Terrarium

Woodland/forest terraria can be utilized for chameleons of humid, rainy montane and tropical origins. Because of the host of easily grown potted houseplants and scientifically formulated soils that are available, woodland/forest terraria are among the most easily constructed and maintained of the various terrarium types. Besides the plants, attractive branches and rocks work well as decorative and functional objects in the woodland/forest terrarium. To successfully maintain your plants, make sure that their roots remain damp, but not soggy,

— T I P —

Warning!

Do not use pine oils or other phenol-based disinfectants for cleaning your chameleon cage. Phenols are absorbed through the skin. Even lingering odors can be deleterious.

and provide them with adequate lighting. Even shade-tolerant philodendrons, pothos, and syngoniums will require several hours of fairly strong light daily if they are to survive.

The basics: When constructing a woodland terrarium, we suggest first placing an inch or two (2.5–5 cm) of pea-sized gravel as the base of the substrate. Atop this, place a thickness or two of air-conditioning filter material. When cut to the exact size of the terrarium, this latter prevents the two or three inches (5–7.5 cm) of soil that comes next from filling the spaces between the gravel. The rocks below the filter material act as a reservoir that will prevent excess water from destroying the roots of your plants if you should happen to overwater. Of course, if you regularly overwater, or overwater too excessively, the reservoir will become full and provide little benefit to the setup.

Some terrarium keepers prefer a simplified approach. With this, several inches of commercially available wood mulch (cypress, aspen, etc., but *not* cedar) is used as the substrate, and the plants that are used remain in their pots, merely sunk to the pot rim in the mulch. This is an easily cleaned arrangement. The mulch can be washed, sterilized, dried, and reused.

Humidity: A glass or plastic top will help retain the high humidity preferred by many of the denizens of these habitats. If the humidity remains too high, it can be reduced by substituting a screen or a combination screen and glass cover for the full glass one. A small fan placed to blow air across the screened top can provide ventilation.

This 40-gallon (151-L) terrarium contains a pair of Jackson's chameleons.

We allow some chameleons to spend the hours of daylight outside in large shrubs. The metal ring prevents them from wandering if they descend to the ground. Take predators into consideration when setting up this type of arrangement.

Cage Furnishings

Cage furnishings for chameleons can be both functional and decorative.

✔ Among the primarily functional examples are such items as synthetic bio-vines.

✔ Some of the more terrestrial chameleons seem to enjoy clambering about on rock formations, prone limbs, etc.

✔ Sturdy vining plants and elevated limbs will provide both perches and visual barriers, as well as adding beauty to the terrarium.

✔ Attractive pieces of dried (sometimes bleached or sandblasted) manzanita, grape, or other gnarled woods are often available at pet shops or from the wild.

If multilayered rock formations are provided, the rocks should be held in place (and together) with a nontoxic adhesive. Silicone aquarium sealant is quite satisfactory for this purpose. If even a single flat rock is placed on the surface of the sand, make certain that it cannot accidentally shift and injure your chameleon. Natural rocks provide better clawholds for your specimens than decorative glass rocks do. If misted, rocks, limbs, and vegetation can all provide drinking stations for your chameleons.

Terrarium Cleanliness

Terrarium cleanliness is one of the most important aspects of successful chameleon husbandry. The substrate should be changed or washed frequently, the perches should be scraped and washed as necessary (or discarded), and all hard surfaces, such as rocks and glass, should be cleaned and sterilized. Water, whether in bowls (with aereators) or in daily mistings, *must* be fresh and clean.

Fortunately, chameleons are not particularly messy animals. Keeping a chameleon cage clean is usually rather easy. To sterilize perches, twigs, rocks, cork bark, and the terrarium itself, a diluted solution of either Ro-Cal or chlorine bleach should be used. After cleaning and sterilizing the items, be sure all are thoroughly rinsed with clean, fresh water.

Terrarium cleanliness will do much to assure the long-term good health of your specimens. Regular cleaning will help prevent the spread of both diseases and parasites. The cleaning of

terraria should be a prominent part of your husbandry regimen.

Lighting and Heating

Terrarium lights can be used not only for their primary purpose of illuminating a cage, but also as a reliable and easily controlled heat source. Rather inexpensive in-line thermostats or rheostats can be installed by electricians. Plug-in timers are readily available at hardware stores.

Other heat sources: Heating pads, heat tapes, and undertank heaters are all easily procured in feed, hardware, or pet stores. By placing one of these beneath one end of the terrarium, you can create a desired thermal gradient.

Ceramic heaters that screw into incandescent sockets are also readily available. Providing a heat source from above, they heat the interior of the terrarium but emit no light. If these are used, it will be necessary to also use terrarium lighting during daylight hours.

Full-spectrum light: Is full-spectrum (UV-producing) lighting necessary for chameleons? If it isn't absolutely necessary, it is at least *very* beneficial. Two wavelengths of UV are produced by full-spectrum bulbs. These are UV-A and UV-B. UV-A has been shown, time and again, to promote natural behavior in reptiles. The findings are equally favorable for UV-B. This latter stimulates the synthesis of vitamin D_3, the presence of which enhances calcium absorption and metabolism.

So, do chameleons require the beneficial UV rays? Well, in the wild most arboreal species

A portrait of a graceful chameleon.

A portrait of an adult spiny chameleon.

regularly avail themselves of the benefits of UV-producing sunlight. Even forest-floor dwellers derive the benefits of UV from reflected sunlight. And with chameleons being as difficult as they are to keep anyway, they should be given every assist possible.

To benefit the chameleons, the full-spectrum fluorescent bulbs must be located only 12 to 18 inches (31–46 cm) away from the animals. Thus a basking perch should be strategically situated in the terrarium.

Besides the fluorescent format, full-spectrum incandescent lightbulbs are now readily available. These latter provide all of the benefits typically ascribed to their fluorescent cousins,

TIP

Free Full-Spectrum Lighting

Unfiltered natural sunlight is unquestionably the best provider of UV. If filtered through regular glass or Plexiglas, most of the UV is removed from natural sunlight. Wire-covered wood frame cages are best suited to take advantage of natural sunlight in outdoor locations.

A word of warning: Do not place glass or Plexiglas terraria in the sunlight. Even in cold weather the glass can concentrate the heat and disable or kill your chameleons.

but they produce a fair amount of heat as well. Therefore, the incandescent fixtures provide not only a portion of the desired UV rays, but a heated basking spot.

This is an adult male carpet chameleon.

Chameleon Sociability

As mentioned earlier, chameleons are among the most solitary and territorial of lizard species. Some persist (in fact, insist!) in living solitary lives punctuated only by occasional visits with the opposite sex for the sole purpose of breeding. Other species seem to exist in the wild in pairs. Still others might be found in loose groupings of a single male and two or more females. No chameleon species could be considered truly communal.

Out of Sight, Out of Mind

In an effort to take better advantage of the seasonally waning hours of sunlight, we repositioned two large cages, each holding a trio of veiled chameleons, *Chamaeleo calyptratus*. Although all were imports, all were well acclimated; all were long-term captives; and all had bred repeatedly. Until the repositioning, the cages had been so distant that there had been no chance for the chameleons of one cage to see those in the other. Each cage was furnished with a small ficus tree, at the top of which the chameleons sunned. On the first day subsequent to the repositioning, we noticed no problems. The cages were separated by 20 feet (6 m), and the views between them from all but the uppermost few inches remained basically obscured.

However, on the second day each male was remaining longer than usual at the top of his respective tree. Neither seemed to avail himself of the sun in the usual manner, both remained for long periods in threat postures, and the color of each was brighter than usual. This was puzzling. Could this really be a response by both to the repositioning of the cages? By the afternoon of the second day, when neither male drank when sprayed, there was cause for concern. If stressed, the health of a chameleon can deteriorate quickly. We sat down and watched the lizards. Almost as soon as all was quiet, both males again clambered to the summits of their trees, paralleled each other, and, although separated by leafy boughs, cage frames, two thicknesses of wire, and 20 feet, began territoriality displays. The problem, and the solution, was now clear. An opaque covering was stapled from the bottom to the top of both cages, and within the hour things were back to normal. By then, both male chameleons had descended somewhat, had drunk, and had accepted food insects. It was a clear case of "out of sight, out of mind."

But had we not known the normal behavior of those lizards well enough to realize that something was radically amiss, the outcome would quite probably have been very different, terminating with the death of at least one and perhaps both of those male veiled chameleons.

Compatible Pairs

If not crowded, one to several adult females may be kept with each male. Although the females are usually somewhat less aggressive toward each other, hierarchies may be formed. You must ascertain that all subordinate specimens continue to feed and drink adequately, are allowed to bask, and are not unduly stressed by the dominant female. Juveniles of both sexes may be

TIP

Separate Males

In captivity, it is usually impossible, and never desirable, to keep more than a single sexually mature male of a given species in each cage. Intraspecific aggression among males can be persistent and can lead to fatalities.

housed together, although growth may be more rapid if only a single specimen is kept per container.

It may be possible to keep two diverse species of chameleons together. For instance, we successfully kept a trio of common chameleons and a trio of carpet chameleons together in one of our large step-in cages. The two species showed no interest in each other. Other combinations are likely to be possible. Experiment, but watch closely for adverse reactions.

Werner's chameleons are becoming more popular in the hobby. Males have three horns and occipital lobes.

WATERING AND FEEDING YOUR CHAMELEON

To safeguard the health of your chameleon, you must provide adequate water and well-nourished insects. In addition, you need to monitor your pet carefully to ensure that it drinks and eats sufficiently.

Most chameleons do not recognize standing water as a drinking source. In nature, they either lap the water that condenses and runs down their casques or they lap dew droplets from leaves. A dish of water at the bottom of their cage is unrecognized as a hydration source. Water must be moving, dangling in droplets from leaves, twigs, or even the terrarium top (or if in a dish, roiled with an air stone), to be recognizable.

Acceptable methods of watering your chameleons are:

✔ Misting (indoors)
✔ Spraying with a hose (outside cages)
✔ Drip systems (indoor or outdoor)
✔ Shallow cage-bottom water dish (water roiled by an aquarium air stone)

A spectacularly beautiful female carpet chameleon walks the aerial highways.

✔ Shallow elevated water dish (water roiled by an aquarium air stone)

You may have to try more than one method until you can observe your lizards drinking on a regular basis.

Misting

If you mist or spray the chameleons, direct the spray upward and allow it to fall on the lizards as rain would. We use spray nozzle and an outside hose to "rain upon" the chameleons in our outside cages. Indoor cages are misted using a simple spray bottle, available at any garden store or drugstore. Tap water and hose water constitute our source of water. The step-in cages are gently sprinkled (twice daily for rainforest species, once daily for desert or savanna species) for a period of several minutes. Each chameleon drinks copiously at nearly every sprinkling.

Drip Method

There is a second, almost as effective method of watering the chameleons in these large cages. Several pinhead-sized holes are placed in the bottom of a large plastic bucket. The bucket is then filled with drinking water and placed atop the cage above the tree, while a large "catch-basin" in the form of a big plant saucer is placed on the floor of the cage, underneath the drip area. (You just need to catch most of the drips to help preserve the structural integrity of your cage.)

The water then drips slowly out of the bucket, falls onto the leaves below, and the chameleons drink the droplets from the leaves. This is another place where the wood/wire construction will stand you in good stead. The water that isn't caught by the basin below the drip bucket merely runs out of the cages, preventing the formation of a quagmire that would be detrimental to the health of your lizard.

The drip-bucket method can also be used in indoor terraria. In a smaller indoor cage it will be even more important to empty the catch-basin daily.

Water Dishes

You could try a water dish on the bottom of your cage with an air stone inserted into the dish to "move" the water, or you could place this water dish up higher in the cage. Be certain it is firmly seated, so it cannot move, if you place it above cage bottom. This may appeal to lizards that are reluctant to descend to the ground to drink. It should be placed where it is easily reachable from the chameleon's favorite perching area.

Watch your chameleon to make sure that it is drinking, no matter which technique you try.

Feeding Your Chameleon

Although most chameleons are basically insectivorous, some larger species will also prey on the nestlings of mice and small birds, and at least one species, the veiled chameleon, consumes a fair amount of foliage, flowers, and, occasionally, fruit.

Provide Variety

It may take some prompting and tempting to get your newly imported chameleon feeding well. Offer it a variety of insects: butterworms, waxworms, giant mealworms, mealworms, crickets, locusts (no lubber grasshoppers though!), roaches, or, in the case of baby or small chameleon species, termites and aphids. Most chameleons quickly tire of one insect species. Providing an adequate diet can be quite a task, but the life of your lizard depends on it.

Persuading your chameleon to feed can take some doing. Once deprived of food and water, whether at the collection site, the wholesalers, or the pet store, some chameleons are reluctant to start feeding again. It will be your responsibility to offer fresh food in such secure and calming surroundings that your chameleon just cannot resist nibbling, and then, once started, readily feeding.

Feed Daily

Despite their perpetually slow-motion lifestyle, chameleons require daily feedings. In large step-in cages, this constitutes no problem. We simply maintain a hundred or so crickets (vitamin/mineral-enhanced insect feed is always available to the insects) in the cages at all times. In addition, a small number of mealworms or waxworms is offered at intervals. Growing plants are always in the cages. Some breeder chameleons have thrived on such a regimen for more than four years.

In smaller cages, glass terraria, or cages where insect diet is not provided, "gut-loaded" insects are offered daily. Those not consumed by the lizards must be removed from the terraria and the insects themselves offered food at the end of the day.

Insect Care

Providing a well-rounded diet for your chameleon involves more than simply offering the lizard crickets and mealworms. You've got to offer it *healthy* insects. This means that you must continually feed your insects, no matter the species, a healthy diet. Offering a poorly nourished insect to your chameleon is a little like feeding it bits of chitin; there's not much nutrition in an insect's exoskeleton. A poorly fed or otherwise unhealthy insect offers little but bulk when fed to a chameleon.

Besides a healthy diet immediately prior to being fed to the chameleons, the insects should occasionally be dusted with a powdered vitamin/mineral supplement. We suggest that this be done about twice weekly. We use such calcium supplements as Miner-all, RepCAL (both a D_3 and Ca supplement), and Osteoform (a broad-spectrum vitamin/mineral supplement). After using these supplements over a period of years, we cannot recommend one over the other.

Gut-Loading Your Insects

"Gut-loading" simply means that the insects you feed your chameleons always have a full gut

A female Usumbara giant three-horned chameleon captures crickets.

of healthy food. Calcium, vitamin D_3, fresh fruit and vegetables, fresh alfalfa and/or bean sprouts, honey, and vitamin/mineral-enhanced chick-laying mash are only a few of the foods that may be considered in gut-loading your insects.

Insect availability: Except for "field plankton," all food insects, even houseflies, are commercially available. Inquire at your local pet store or search the classified sections of reptile magazines or the Internet for sources. Buying food insects certainly takes less time than raising them, but either method is acceptable.

Vegetable Matter

The fresh flowers of nasturtium, hibiscus, dandelion, and rose are often eagerly accepted by some chameleons. That these lizards will consume blossoms, and even young leaves, is not well publicized. Do not be afraid to experiment with your chameleons. The diet of some of our large veiled chameleons consisted of large amounts of vegetation. Housed in outside walk-in cages in which potted shrubs grew, both juveniles and adults of these big chameleons ate considerable quantities of hibiscus and ficus leaves as well as insects and the offered blossoms of other plants.

YOUR CHAMELEON'S HEALTH

Despite your care in selection, your chameleon may be ill even before you acquire it. New imports frequently suffer from something as simple but pervasive as dehydration and parasites. Learn to recognize these problems and address them immediately.

Hydration Chambers

The uses and benefits of hydration chambers have long been understood by zoos and other public institutions. They are only now coming into general use by private herpetoculturists and hobbyists to rehydrate chameleons that have become dessicated. They are especially useful for new imports. To reverse advanced dehydration, you will need to do more for the lizards than just sprinkle water into their cage. A rehydration chamber, which is fairly easy to set up, may be in order. The results can be dramatic.

The term "hydration chamber" is merely a highfalutin way of saying "rain chamber." But there is nothing highfalutin about the rain chamber's value to the herpetoculturist. These receptacles can make the difference between

Male Poroto Mountain chameleons are Triceratops lookalikes.

life and death for dehydrated chameleons (or any other reptiles or amphibians). They also can be the seasonal trigger for breeding behavior.

Simply put, a hydration chamber provides a recognizable and continuous source of water to the animal. It can be a closed system of high humidity or a wood and wire cage with a drip watering system. Which you use depends on your circumstances and the condition of the animal.

In Florida, a warm area of ambient high humidity, the latter system works well. New chameleons that are dessicated will spend the majority of their daylight hours hidden among the leaves of the drip-laden ficus, their skins shiny from water droplets, their most evident movement a regular swallowing. As they become rehydrated, the chameleons will begin exploring their cage, sunning during the day and returning each morning to the top of their

cage, near the drip system. In an area where outdoor caging is not practical, a self-contained hydration tank will work just as well.

Making Your Own

Outdoor caging can be modified to a hydration chamber simply by using a mist nozzle on the end of a hose fixed over the cage. Run fresh water through this for an hour or more a day onto the plants within the cage.

An indoor hydration chamber can be made from an aquarium, a circulating water pump, branches and a privacy plant (a small philodendron works well here), a tank heater, a small plastic water bucket with drip holes, and a screen or hardware cloth top.

Stand the pump upright in one corner of the tank and lay the heater along the bottom of the tank. Put enough water in the tank to cover the heater and the intake of the recirculating pump, about 3 inches (7 cm). Bend a piece of 1/2- or 1/4-inch (0.5–1 cm) hardware cloth to form a false bottom over the water and the heater (you'll have to notch it around

Stressed Usumbara giant three-horned chameleons become more strongly banded, and the peppering of dark spots contrasts sharply with the ground color.

the corner pump), so that if your chameleon falls or clambers down, it won't end up in the water. Install the branches and the plant atop the false bottom. Bend a second piece of hardware cloth to form a top, notching if needed for the circulating pump.

Position the small drip bucket adjacent to the pump, and place the outflow of the pump into the drip bucket. If you poke a hole through the bucket to firmly seat the outflow tube, you'll have fewer "fallout" problems.

Testing and Use

Plug in the pump and heater, and check the system before you install the lizards. The heater should keep the water at about 80°F (27°C), and the pump should circulate the warmed water from the bottom of the tank into the drip bucket. A continuous warmed flow of "rainwater" should drip from the bucket onto the branches and leaves below. A light can be positioned over the tank to offer illumination and a basking area.

Place your lizard inside the tank and observe it and the tank for a few moments. Needless to say, because you are recirculating the water, it must be changed every time the tank is used. It will do your lizard no good to be doused with contaminated drinking water.

A two- to four-hour period in the hydration tank goes a long way toward rehydrating your lizard. You may need to use several daily sessions until your lizard is no longer dehydrated and (with luck) is feeding well in its own cage. Remember to use fresh water, and keep the tank temperature at about 80°F (27°C) with a warmer basking area.

Respiratory Diseases

The good news is that well-acclimated, properly maintained chameleons are not prone to respiratory ailments. The bad news is that any stressed chameleon, whether a new import, a marginally healthy specimen, or one subjected to unnatural periods of cold (especially humid low temperatures), may break down with a cold or pneumonia. Some respiratory infections may also be associated with the weakening brought about by an untenably heavy endoparasitic burden.

Most respiratory ailments, however, are attributable to stress.

Prevention Measures

We already know that chameleons can be difficult to maintain. Curing a sick one is even

====== TIP ======

Worth Repeating

Why use a hydration chamber? The use of these or similar units can do much to help moisture-deprived reptiles recuperate. Those that will most benefit from such a structure are the rainforest species that are freighted long distances to reach the pet markets of America, Asia, Europe, and other countries. Chameleons are particularly vulnerable to dehydration during shipping. If rehydrated promptly and fully, many that would otherwise die can be saved.

Female Usumbara giant three-horned chameleons lack horns.

TIP

A Cautionary Note

Simply stated, the treatment for endoparasites involves administering a potentially toxic substance into the system of your chameleon. Because of this, dosages of the medication *must* be exact, and even then a weakened lizard might not survive the treatment. Again, we strongly suggest you avail yourself of the services of a knowledgeable veterinarian.

more tricky. Here are some suggestions to lessen the possibility of respiratory illness occurring:

✔ Cage your chameleon properly; prevent drafts.

✔ If kept with a cagemate, make sure they are compatible.

✔ Deparasitize your chameleon.

✔ Keep the cage temperature within the acceptable norms at all times. In northern climes have a backup system in place.

✔ Feed your chameleon a proper diet.

Respiratory ailments are initially accompanied by sneezing, lethargic demeanor, and unnaturally rapid, often shallow breathing.

As the respiratory disorder worsens, rasping and bubbling may accompany each of your chameleon's breaths. The animal is extremely uncomfortable. At this stage the respiratory infection is often critical and can be fatal. Have your chameleon examined and treated by your veterinarian while there's a chance the treatment will be successful.

Treatment Options

There are many "safe" drugs available, but some respiratory diseases do not respond well to these. The newer aminoglycoside drugs are more effective but correspondingly more dangerous. There is little latitude in dosage amounts, and the chameleon *must* be well hydrated to ensure against renal (kidney) damage. The injection site for aminoglycosides must be *anterior* to mid-body to assure that the renal portal system is not compromised. It is mandatory that your veterinarian be well acquainted with reptilian medicine to assure that the correct decisions are made.

It is vital that basking temperatures be elevated during treatment. As soon as a respiratory ailment is suspected, elevate the temperature of your chameleon's basking area to 88–94°F (31–35°C). Do not elevate the temperature of the entire cage, just the basking area. The ambient cage temperature should be 82–86°F (27–29°C).

Endoparasites

The presence of internal parasites in wild-caught chameleons is a foregone conclusion. Among others that may be present are roundworms, pin-worms, nematodes, filarids, tapeworms, and a whole host of flagellate protozoans.

To Treat or Not?

Although many people feel that wholesale worming of all imported chameleons is a necessity, we feel that whether or not the parasites are combated vigorously should depend on the behavior of the lizard itself. Certainly the problems created by endoparasitic loads in

The stump-tailed leaf chameleon is the most frequently seen member of this group.

weakened chameleons need to be addressed promptly. Will treating a wild import for worms cause it more stress than the presence of the worms themselves? That's a hard question to answer. A fecal exam will have to be run to determine what parasites the chameleon is actually harboring in its gut. Your reptile veterinarian is your best guide in cases like this, but the decision is a judgment call.

However, if the specimen in question is bright-eyed, alert, feeding well, and has good color, you may wish to forego an immediate veterinary assessment. Endoparasitic loads can actually diminish if you keep the cage of your specimen scrupulously clean, thereby preventing reinfestation.

Subcutaneous nematodes are prevalent in many species of chameleons. These parasites are easily seen as they traverse between the skin and the muscular tissues of the chameleons. They also migrate to and from the gastrointestinal tract. Certain chameleon species seem more susceptible to these parasites than others. Four of the most commonly imported chameleon species are quite apt to harbor fair numbers of subcutaneous nematodes. These species are the Senegal (*C. senegalensis*), the graceful (*C. gracilis*), and the flap-necked (*C. dilepis*) chameleons of Africa and the panther chameleon (*F. pardalis*) of Madagascar. Avoid any chameleons with these nematode problems. What you are seeing beneath the skin is the proverbial tip of the iceberg.

Ectoparasites

External parasites are less problematic to treat than endoparasites. Only two kinds, ticks and mites, are seen with any degree of

Elliott's mountain chameleon is only infrequently seen and is often of rather dull coloration.

regularity. Both ticks and mites feed on the body fluids of their hosts. Both are easily overlooked.

Ticks: Ticks are the larger of the two, deflated and seedlike when empty, rounded and bladderlike when engorged. It is best if they are removed singly whenever seen. They embed their mouthparts deeply when feeding, and if merely pulled from the lizard, these may break off in the wound. It is best to first dust them individually with Sevin powder or rub their body parts with rubbing alcohol, then return a few minutes later and pull the ticks gently off with a pair of tweezers.

Mites: Thanks to the advent of No-Pest Strips (2.2 dichlorovinyl dimethyl phosphate), mites are easily managed. A small square (approximately 3/4 × 3/4 inch [2 × 2 cm]) placed in the chameleon tank (out of reach of the lizard) for from 12 to 24 hours will usually kill all adult mites. If some survive the initial treatment, treat again a day later. No-Pest does not destroy mite

eggs. Therefore it will be necessary to repeat the entire treatment nine days later. A dilute Ivermectin spray or commercially available anti-mite sprays are also quickly effective.

Edema/Vitamin A Excess

Just as we thought we were edging out ahead of the game in solving chameleon husbandry problems, a new problem—edema—began to manifest itself. Edema is the accumulation of fluids subcutaneously. In humans, there are a variety of causes, all serious. The more we learn about edema in chameleons, the more we realize that it is only a symptom of a bigger problem. Edema is frequently fatal.

A portrait of an adult male high-casqued chameleon.

This male high-casqued chameleon is in a defensive pose.

Symptoms and Causes

Edema is characterized by goiter-like swellings in the neck and throat. Even long-term captives were developing these symptoms. What was the cause? What could be done?

As hobbyists and researchers compared notes, vitamin A became suspect. And, indeed, an excess of vitamin A may well be a con-tributing, or even the primary, agent.

But it would appear that vitamin A, by itself, does *not* cause edema. Rather, it would seem that the noticeable fluid pockets are the result of organ dysfunction. The kidneys, the liver, and the heart have all been suggested. Thus, edema is an outwardly visible symptom of a far more serious underlying problem.

It would seem that an excess of supplemental vitamins (perhaps A, perhaps A and others) does figure in the problem somewhere. And since an excess of vitamin A is known to cause liver and kidney damage, it might behoove herpetocul-turists to reduce the amount of A offered sup-plementally. Do not eliminate vitamin A com-pletely; remember that a lack of vitamin A is also fatal. Administer your vitamin/mineral supplements wisely. A new reptile vitamin supplement now on the market contains beta-carotene rather than vitamin A.

TIP

Preventive Measure

You can forestall hypervitaminosis by gut-loading your food insects with beta-carotene rich foods. This may be the best way of all to supply vitamin A to your chameleons. Chameleons fed carotene-enriched crickets can synthesize their own vitamin A.

BREEDING CHAMELEONS

Most chameleons show sexual differences (sexual dimorphism). The males often display prominent secondary characteristics such as horns, rostral protuberances, tarsal spurs, or crests. Males are also often larger than the females. Sex-linked color differences may also occur in some species.

Sexing Your Chameleon

In those species that do not exhibit overt sexual differences, gender can often be determined by examining the base of the tail immediately posterior to the cloaca. If the specimen is a male, a bilateral swelling caused by the hemipenes may often be seen, one swelling on each side of the ventral tail base.

The Function of Color

True chameleons depend on their color-changing abilities to advertise many emotions. Defending territories calls for males to display their most brilliant colors from the most visible platforms. Yemen veiled chameleons, for instance, ascend to the tips of the highest branches in tamarind trees, assume their most

A nesting female veiled chameleon will peer frequently from her in-progress nest. Chameleons are the most vulnerable to predators at this time.

brilliantly contrasting hues of gold and turquoise, and visibly dare another of their own sex and species to approach.

The displays serve a second purpose as well—that of advertising a virile and successful male to any females within eyeshot. However, it is not only the males that use color and pattern to advertise sexuality and other moods. The colors and patterns of the females are also indicators. One color advertises sexual nonreceptivity. Another advertises receptivity and yet another announces, "I've been bred, I'm gravid; go away!"

Species Identity

Display colors vary by species. After a cool starlit night, the rising desert sun begins its journey above the horizon. First light, then warmth begin to infiltrate the desert coolness. With the increasing light and warmth a sleeping male veiled chameleon stirs. He has spent the night soundly sleeping, his body parallel to the twig to which he is tightly clinging. The rays of the sun are now reaching him, but

there is little warmth to be quickly gotten. Slowly, independently swiveling eyes survey the landscape. All is quiet, but the cold has slowed his movement and left him at his most vulnerable. Convinced that no danger is lurking, the chameleon slowly alters his position and flattens his body. Now, with the axis of his body exactly perpendicular to the warming rays, he begins to warm—but not quickly enough.

The light and heat literally bounce from the yellow and blue of his body. But soon the light and the heat provide a new stimulus. Within moments the chameleon's color has darkened. He is now deep blackish blue and deep ochre. Rather than being reflected, the warming rays are now absorbed and utilized. The chameleon is soon warm enough. His color lightens, and he again faces the sun, now presenting as little body mass as possible to the rays. The rays again bounce harmlessly off his scales.

The challenge: The lizard ascends. Just before gaining the top, he notices the sun

A pair of Senegal chameleons breed in a tree.

reflecting from something atop a shrub a short distance away. The bright blues and yellow reflect like a semaphore—another male veiled chameleon. This cannot be ignored.

The vanquished: The colors of our hero intensify. The pretty blue and yellow give way to brighter hue, and slowly, hand over hand, foot over foot, he begins his ascent again. The desert warms, the light brightens, the sun is now nearly overhead. Each male displays, then displays again. Finally, number two, slightly smaller and slightly duller, folds under the stare and continued display of number one, descends and moves to another shrub further away. Number one watches him go, ceases his own display, and, with his territory again unthreatened, begins to forage. Had number two remained where first seen, the possibility of additional display, stylized bluffs, and actual skirmish existed.

The victor: But as number one forages, hoping to assuage his hunger, another chameleon is seen. However, this one is green and has a low crest. It's a female. At about the same time, the new interloper sees the male. Again colors change. The male reassumes his brightest livery and the female brightens some, indicating sexual receptivity. The courtship is quick and to the point, and soon the pair parts. The female may breed another time or two within the next few days, but soon physiological changes occur that tell her at least one of the breedings was successful. Her eggs have begun to develop, shell formation will soon begin, and there is no longer a need to breed to assure the continuation of the line.

Female Behavior: From that point, for the several weeks until the female chameleon lays her clutch of 30 to 60 eggs, she is entirely unreceptive, even hostile, to the advances of any males encountered. Her base color changes and she takes on a brown to brownish-green ground color. Orange dots, dashes, or figures, oriented vertically on the flanks, separate the ground color into broad bands. The ground color is broken dorsally by bands of blue or turquoise.

Gravid Coloration

A gravid female veiled chameleon is a very different-appearing lizard from a nongravid one. As the egg deposition date nears, the female becomes increasingly brilliant. This is of considerable significance to lizards as visually oriented as chameleons. They are advertisement colors that tell the males she is not available. Should a male chance to question

the colors, he is greeted with huffs, puffs, and gaping jaws, and if he is indiscreet enough to continue his advances, savage bites from the female quickly deter him.

Egg Deposition

Finally the deposition day arrives and, digging a deep hole (sometimes a foot [30 cm] or slightly more), the female lays her clutch. There the eggs will incubate, subjected to the vagaries of nature, for several months. The completion of the task—the initial digging, the actual laying, and the refilling and tamping down of the soil—may take a full day. One female that we retained would construct her hole on the first day, lay sometime during the night, and busily fill the hole for much of the second day.

After the egg laying, the female emerges, much exhausted and now dully colored. As

A 2-week-old flap-necked chameleon poses for its picture.

soon as the covering of the eggs is completed, she returns to the shrubs to hunt and, if she is lucky enough for the dew to be heavy, drink. It is important at this stage that the body fluids expended in egg deposition be quickly replaced.

Within a day or so, the female chameleon again assumes her nongravid livery. If she sees a male, and if he sees her, the sequence is replayed.

Gravid Female Coloration

Female panther chameleons, *Furcifer pardalis*, of most populations are a rather unspectacular brownish-gray or brownish-green color when not gravid. Egg-carrying females intensify in color soon after breeding and within a week or two have assumed a deep brown coloration highlighted by large, light dorsolateral "portholes." As the deposition date nears, the portholes change to intense fiery orange.

When gravid, the normally pale female carpet chameleon, *Furcifer lateralis*, assumes a pattern so complex that it beggars description. The highlights are yellow and rose suffused over straw and brown.

The advertisement colors are truly of importance in these slow-moving, visually oriented arboreal creatures. You need only to observe the interactions of several chameleons for a short time to determine exactly how important the colors are.

Dominant chameleons are brilliantly colored. Subordinate ones are dull to the point of obscurity. Nongravid females show enticement—or if not enticement, at least receptivity—through their colors. Egg-laden females advertise their nonreceptivity with screaming gaudiness.

It is little wonder that chameleons are creatures of intrigue to so many hobbyists and researchers! What is important is that the messages of color be correctly understood and interpreted.

Cycling Defined

Although many people consider keeping a chameleon hale and hearty a sufficient challenge, many of us wish to breed our lizards. While not easy, if compatible chameleons are kept in large enough facilities and are "cycled" properly, successfully completing this objective is far from impossible. The term "cycled," as used here, pertains to the preparations—climatic, light duration, and others—that you should make to ready your chameleons for breeding.

Role of External Stimuli

The breeding sequences of most reptiles and amphibians are at least partially triggered by external stimuli. Among these stimuli, seasonal temperature changes, seasonal humidity changes, and photoperiods are prominent. Indeed, certain temperate-climate reptiles cannot be successfully bred unless they are subjected to a period of chilling and darkness similar to their periods of brumation (hibernation). Many chameleons are tropical creatures that do not undergo extended periods of dormancy; those species from Europe and the higher mountainous regions of Africa and Madagascar are the exception. But all areas experience certain annual climatic changes. These seasonal changes include reduced hours of daylight, lower nighttime temperatures, reduced relative humidity, and decreased rain.

Panther chameleons are geographically variable in color, but collection data is often not supplied to importers.

The climatic changes are even less dramatic in the more tropical areas, being largely limited to a reduction of humidity and shower activity during the winter months.

Internal Reactions

Slight though these changes may be, they play a profound role in the life cycle of the chameleon. During the periods of reduced light, temperature, humidity, and rainfall, the chameleon decreases production of certain key hormones, which causes ovarian and testicular regression. With the lengthening days and correspondingly increasing warmth, humidity, and rain activity, hormonal production again increases, stimulating interest in reproduction. With the increase in the production of testosterone also comes increased interest in territoriality with a correspondingly increased aggressive attitude toward rival males. It is at this time that hostility toward other chameleons increases.

Courtship

The courtship of a female chameleon by a male is characterized by stylized body language (rather similar to that used in territoriality displays) and color displays. Adult males are considerably larger than adult females. The body language involves pushups, head bobs and nods, and repeated dewlap distensions. After the whirlwind courtship the male will mount a receptive female, retaining position by grasping her nape with his jaws. The male will curve and angle his body around that of the female until their cloacae are juxtaposed. When their bodies are correctly positioned, intromission is usually quickly accomplished and is accompanied by a varied series of movements, including a "shrugging" sequence. After breeding is completed, the chameleons again go their separate ways.

In the wild, chameleons are opportunistic breeders throughout the late winter and early spring months. Being loners, when the paths of two receptive chameleons of the opposite sex cross during those months, more often than not they will breed. A successful breeding will result in eggs within eight weeks, or live young in several months.

Nesting

For an egg-laying species, site preparation is important. After choosing a suitable site, the female will use her forefeet to dig deeply into the earth. Loosened dirt and debris are removed with the rear feet. When finished the hole will often be big enough to completely hide the female while she is laying. Usually, several times during the preparations, the female will reverse her head-down position and peer quizzically

from the deepening depression, perhaps scouting for approaching danger. Certainly during nest preparation, she is more vulnerable to predation than at almost any other time in her life.

The nesting efforts may be curtailed at any time during the preparation. If disturbed by a predator or if the digging is thwarted by a maze of roots or rocks, the female will often leave to begin anew elsewhere at another time. Even if the nest is completed after several periods of digging interspersed with periods of rest, the female, based upon criteria known best to her, may deem the nesting chamber unsuitable. Should this be the case, the female will abandon the completed but unused nest and proceed anew at another location and another time.

However, if all is deemed well with the initial excavation, the female will, after a period of rest, lay and position each egg of her clutch, then fill the hole with the removed dirt and leave. Dependent on temperature and moisture, the period of incubation can and will vary considerably. At the low end, under ideal nest conditions, the eggs may hatch in about six months. Under cooler, drier conditions, the incubation duration may near a full 22 months.

Captive Breeding

Now let's talk about breeding captive pet chameleons. We will discuss two methods, one suitable for the benign climates of the lower Rio Grande Valley, southern Florida, and southern California where chameleons are often kept in outdoor settings, and a second method suitable for chameleons kept indoors in any climate.

This gravid female veiled chameleon is digging her foot-deep (30 cm) nest.

The color and pattern indicate that this female carpet chameleon is gravid.

To successfully breed your chameleons, you—and they—must meet several criteria.

✔ The most important of these, of course, is to have a sexual pair.

✔ The pair needs to be temporarily compatible.

✔ Once successfully bred, the female needs to have a deposition chamber in which to lay her clutch.

✔ You need the knowledge and facilities to hatch the viable eggs that are laid.

Besides these basics, the use of several additional stimulatory cues may help you achieve your goal.

Preparations

We will assume that you do, in fact, have a pair of chameleons. "Tame," content, and healthy chameleons make the best breeders. If your chameleons are fearful and skittish, breeding sequences are easily interrupted.

Have your incubator set to the proper humidity and temperature before actually having to use it. Remember that chameleon eggs literally like it cool.

Outdoor facilities: Chameleons kept outdoors in the southernmost areas of the United States can be allowed to breed and nest nearly like they would in the wild. We, as owners, merely need to ensure that suitable nesting areas are present in their cages. If the cage sits directly on the ground, the female chameleon will dig her nesting chamber into the ground.

Indoors: If the chameleon cage does not rest on the ground, or if your cage is indoors, you'll need to provide a large bucket of dampened sand as a nest-digging site.

Once the eggs have been laid, you'll need to remove and incubate them.

Inducing Reproduction

Although hobbyists now know more about the keeping and breeding of chameleons than ever before, there remains much more to learn.

Here are some pointers. Certain aspects may vary by species or even population (high elevation cool versus low elevation warm).

In their rapidly changing color and pattern, common chameleons epitomize the variability typical of many chameleons.

The reproductive biology of even warm-habitat chameleons is affected by the seasons. The term "seasons" may indicate either those that we in temperate climates consider normal (spring, summer, autumn, winter) or the less well-defined but equally important periods of rain versus comparative dryness of the equatorial regions.

In either case, seasonal adjustments of temperature, humidity, and in some cases photoperiod have appeared effective in inducing spermatogenesis/ovulation in chameleons.

To cycle chameleons from north or south of the equator:

✔ Reduce normal daytime and nighttime temperatures by several degrees.

✔ Continue to provide a hot spot (warmed basking area) but for a lesser number of hours daily.

✔ Reduce food availability somewhat. This is especially important if your chameleons become largely quiescent. When food is offered, small meals of smaller-than-usual insects will be best.

✔ Reduce relative humidity, actual dampness, and hours of illumination (photoperiod) for 60 to 90 days.

To cycle chameleons from within a few degrees of the equator:

✔ Proceed as above, but a reduction of the photoperiod may not be as critical.

✔ Reduce both the relative and actual humidity somewhat. This can be accomplished by increasing the ventilation of your cage while reducing the amount of water used in everyday maintenance.

✔ Increase to normal proportions after 60 to 90 days.

Live-bearers

Although the greatest number of chameleon species are oviparous (egg-layers), a fair number of species retain the eggs until they develop fully internally, and so give birth to living young, each contained in a transparent membranous sac.

Incubation and Sexual Maturity

Baby chameleons do grow quickly. It is possible for them to attain sexual maturity in less time than it took them to hatch.

Species	Clutch Size	Incubation Duration (in months)	Time to Attain Sexual Maturity (in months)
Bradypodion fischeri	6–22	7–10	6
Chamaeleo calyptratus	15–70	7–8	6
Chamaeleo chamaeleon	12–70	10	8
Chamaeleo gracilis	10–40	6–7	5–6
Chamaeleo hoehnelii	4–22	n/a	5
Chamaeleo jacksonii	8–32	n/a	6
Chamaeleo johnstoni	5–35	7–10	5–6
Chamaeleo montium	4–25	5–7	4–5
Furcifer pardalis	10–50	6–7	5–7
Furcifer lateralis	5–30	6–7	3

Of these ovoviviparous species, the Jackson's chameleon, *Chamaeleo jacksonii* ssp. from Africa, is most frequently seen in the United States. Other live-bearing forms are the little two-striped *C. bitaeniatus* and the high-casqued *C. hoehneli*, both of Africa, as well as many of the southern African members of the genus *Bradypodion* (often called dwarf chameleons).

Several of these ovoviviparous chameleon species have been bred for many generations in captivity, especially in Europe where herpetoculturists have concentrated on the captive breeding of these interesting creatures.

Temperatures

It is particularly important that gravid female ovoviviparous chameleons be provided a temperature regimen that is suitable for the development of the babies. Although the terrarium can be "cool" at night (65–72°F [18–22°C]) with warmer day temperatures (74–80°F [23–27°C]), a somewhat warmer basking spot will allow the female to increase her body temperature above that of the ambient should she choose. Overhead, warmth-producing lighting (full-spectrum incandescent bulbs) is best for this purpose when natural sunlight is not available.

Neonates

The neonates are enclosed in a very thin membranous sac that adheres easily to most dry substrates. As the babies are expelled, the female chameleon often presses her vent against the branch or perch to which she is clinging. The enclosing sacs adhere to the branch, and the babies will usually burst free in a few minutes.

Females may also merely drop the babies on the substrate. It seems that the sudden stop galvanizes the babies to action, and they immediately begin their efforts to escape the sac. It is thought that a greater percentage of babies emerge from the dropped birth sacs than from the attached ones. Since contact with the air quickly dries and solidifies the sac, babies that don't emerge within the first few minutes will have an increasingly difficult time in emerging. If humidity is low, the sacs dry quite quickly. In the wild, babies that fail to emerge will die. In captivity, if you are present when the babies are born, you can assist any of the weaker ones out of their sacs. However, they may not survive even with a human assist.

Timing

The young of these ovoviviparous species are usually born during the daylight hours. The ambient temperature may dictate to a degree when the females give birth. The females seem to choose the temperature at which the babies will be most active. It is possible that a cool temperature may inhibit the birthing event for a day or even more—until the return of suitable conditions.

Some ovoviviparous chameleon species produce large litters of young. The clutches of a Jackson's chameleon can number from 10 to 50, in contrast to the 3 to 12 young per litter produced by many of the dwarf chameleons.

Egg-Layers

Several weeks after successfully breeding, captive chameleons of oviparous (egg-laying) species will begin to seek a suitable egg deposition site. If such a site is not regularly available within the cage, it must be provided. Most chameleons dig deep nests. This seems especially true of species from seasonally or perpetually arid habitats. In nature, deeper layers of the substrate retain the moisture content necessary to prevent egg desiccation better than shallower ones.

Nests

Even when captive, chameleons continue to dig deep nests. Female veiled chameleons dig nests a full foot (30 cm) in depth, stopping only when they encounter the bottom of the nesting pail. The nest of the common

Prehensile tail curled tightly, this neonate two-striped chameleon warily eyes the camera.

The horns of neonate Mt. Kenya Jackson's chameleons are represented by nubs.

chameleon may be 8 inches (20 cm) deep and that of the female panther chameleon about 10 inches (25 cm). Female carpet chameleons have dug nests that vary from a minimal surface depression in which the eggs are barely covered to a nest about 3 inches (7.5 cm) deep. Leaf chameleons may simply lay their eggs in damp surface vegetation.

We feel it is best to allow female chameleons to complete the entire nesting sequence, from digging and readying the nest to laying and refilling the deposition burrow.

Female chameleons will advertise their readiness to lay. They will depart from their normal pattern of behavior by descending to the floor of the cage and wandering nervously about. At that time they must be provided with a nesting site. We keep the nesting bucket brightly illuminated with an overhead bulb. When so illuminated, the female will continue to dig throughout the night. When the bucket is not lighted, the female will often rest during most of the hours of darkness. The female is prevented from escaping by placing a covered wire-mesh sleeve around the bucket.

The entire nesting sequence can take up to 24 hours.

The nesting area is merely a 5-gallon (19-L) pail filled to the brim with a suitably moistened sand/soil mixture. The mixture contains just enough moisture to keep the nesting burrow from collapsing while the female is digging. If the soil is gently tamped after mixing and moistening, the walls of the nesting burrow will have more structural integrity.

After the female has completed the nesting sequence and left the site, we carefully dig up and remove the eggs to a more controllable area for incubation.

Incubation

Chameleon eggs are usually incubated in covered plastic deli cups. The substrate we prefer is either barely moistened vermiculite or barely moistened unmilled sphagnum moss. We have found that both work well.

A hatchling panther chameleon shies away from the camera.

The eggs of many of the chameleons that incubate at cool temperatures seem to include a diapause (a temperature/humidity-induced cessation of development) in their incubation cycle. The diapause often occurs during the driest or coolest part of the cycle. It may be necessary to simulate the diapause when eggs are being artificially incubated.

Eggs of most lowland/desert chameleons, which normally incubate at fairly warm temperatures, are not subject to a diapause.

If you are unsure of the temperature at which to incubate your chameleon's eggs, err on the side of coolness.

The eggs are usually divided into several groups, each group in a separate cup. This is merely a safeguard should incubation conditions deteriorate in one egg container.

The number of eggs in a clutch can vary from one or two with the smallest of the leaf chameleons to more than 80 with the fecund veiled chameleon.

Temperatures

Incubation temperatures vary tremendously but are always cooler than what you would feel was good for the eggs. The eggs of some of the montane species incubate well at 63 to 68°F (17–20°C). The eggs of some of the lowland and desert forms will withstand temperatures of 80 to 82°F (27–29°C). To determine what temperatures should be used, it is important that you know the exact species of chameleon with which you are working and, if it is a species that ranges widely in altitude (and hence temperature), from where in its range the specimen came.

The Incubation Process

Why is the incubation duration so lengthy? Chameleons have adapted to some of the more inhospitable microhabitats within the tropics and subtropics of the Old World. Their activity patterns are often slowed or even halted by periods of drought or cold. In montane areas—even in the tropics—the cold can last for several weeks. There are some areas where soil temperatures never reach 70°F (21°C).

Many chameleon eggs, laid at the beginning of good weather, develop quickly for the few weeks of good weather, then enter a diapause brought about by cooling or drying soil conditions. The embryonic development largely stops for what may be a lengthy period. Continued development is brought about by a warming or rehydrating of the soil.

By the time embryonic development is complete, the tiny seasonal insects that will be so badly needed to fuel the rapid growth of hatchling chameleons are again abundant.

In each of the species accounts on page 53 have included suggested incubation lengths. The eggs of most species that incubate for more than six months experience a diapause. With some species the optimum temperature and humidity during diapause remain unknown. Please record your successes and failures and make the information available to other hobbyists; chameleon interest groups and publications are listed in Information.

Care of Eggs

When your chameleon has laid its eggs, remove them from the nest as soon as possible. When you move the eggs, make sure you do not turn them. Keep the same side upward at all times. With some types of reptiles, the position of the air pocket inside the egg cannot change once the egg has been laid. If the egg is rolled over, the air pocket moves and the embryo suffocates.

The eggs of chameleons are soft-shelled and permeable. They are capable of both desiccating and overhydrating. Therefore, incubation conditions need to be fairly precise. Place the eggs in a series of containers, which in turn will be placed inside the incubator. Incubation is a simple but exacting process that involves keeping the eggs at the proper warmth and humidity.

Both vermiculite and sphagnum make good incubation media. The vermiculite should be moistened with four parts of water to six parts

After a lengthy incubation, a baby veiled chameleon greets the world.

of vermiculite, by weight. After it is thoroughly mixed, the eggs may be placed directly on, or half buried in, the dampened vermiculite. A shallow, open dish of water in the incubator will help keep the relative humidity at 100 percent. If sphagnum is used, it should be thoroughly moistened, then squeezed as dry as possible by hand. The eggs can be nestled directly in the moss. If the moss or vermiculite is too dry or too wet, the eggs will desiccate or overhydrate, respectively. Both conditions can be fatal to the developing embryo.

It seems best to keep each egg separated from its nearest neighbor by about an inch (2.5 cm). If the eggs are in contact with one another, the entire clutch, including those still slightly premature, may hatch simultaneously. Well-separated eggs are not apt to do this, hatching instead when development is complete.

Most feed stores sell Styrofoam hen's egg incubators that will hold several deli cups of eggs and that are suitable for the incubation of chameleon eggs.

Making an incubator is relatively easy. You'll need the following:

✔ A wafer thermostat/heater
✔ A thermometer
✔ A Styrofoam cooler with thick sides (a fish shipping box is ideal)
✔ A heat tape or hanging heating coil
✔ An electrical cord and wall plug
✔ 3 wire nuts
✔ A heavy wire shelf to hold egg containers 1 to 2 inches (2.5–5 cm) above the coiled heat tape

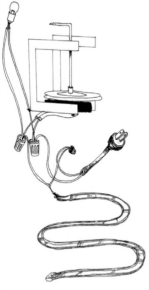

Use a wafer thermostat and a heat tape to make your own incubator.

Your goal is to wire the wafer thermostat into the circuitry between the heat-transmitting unit and the electrical cord. This will allow you to regulate the temperature of your incubator. Then follow these steps:

1. Cut the electrical cord (not the heat tape!) about 1 foot (30 cm) from the heat tape. If you use a heating coil, two short electrical leads will be protruding. Do not cut these.

2. Poke a hole through the lid of the Styrofoam cooler and suspend the thermostat/heater from the inside. Add another hole for a thermometer so you can check the inside temperature without opening the top. If there's no flange on the thermometer to keep it from slipping through the hole in the lid, use a rubber band wound several times around the thermometer to form a flange.

3. Poke a hole through the side of the Styrofoam container just large enough to run the electrical wire through.

4. Pull the electrical cord through the side of the incubator.

5. Suspend the heating coil from the top of the incubator,

or coil the heat tape loosely on the bottom.

6. Remove about 1/2 inch (1.3 cm) of insulation from the cut ends of both cords, and separate the wires about 4 inches (10 cm) back from the cut ends.

7. While carefully following the directions that come with the wafer thermostat and using a wire nut, connect one of the wire leads extending from the heating unit (coil or tape) to the designated red lead extending from the thermostat.

8. Use another wire nut to connect the remaining lead of the thermostat to one of the exposed leads from the wall plug section of the wire.

9. Use the third wire nut to connect the remaining free end of the wall plug section to the remaining unattached lead of the heat tape.

10. Put the lid onto the cooler and plug in the thermostat/heater.

11. Wait half an hour and check the temperature. Adjust the thermostat/heater by using the L pin (the rheostat) on the top of the thermostat until the incubator attains the temperature you desire.

12. Once you have regulated the temperature, put

INCUBATOR

the egg container holding shelf in place inside the incubator, place the container of eggs onto the shelf, and close the lid.

You'll need to monitor both the temperature and the humidity. The preferred humidity is 90 to 100 percent. This can be accomplished by keeping the hatching medium of peat and soil damp to the touch but too dry to squeeze out any water with your hand. The normal temperature range of chameleon eggs varies by species between 68 and 80°F (20–27°C). Check the species accounts in the following pages for the suggested temperature. Chameleon eggs are quite unlike the eggs of most other lizards in incubation durations. Some may take over 15 months to hatch and may require a diapause, a period when the embryo growth is slowed or halted.

Check the incubator temperature daily and add a little water to the incubating medium as needed. You'll need to remove the eggs with obvious problems, like fuzzy mold, but since the eggs aren't touching each other, the other eggs won't be spoiled.

If the eggs are infertile, they may show obvious signs of spoiling in one to several weeks. As mentioned above, discard spoiled eggs. Those that are fertile will remain white and turgid to the touch.

Even after slitting their eggs in preparation for emergence (pipping), the babies are really in no hurry to leave the egg. They may look out and decide to stay inside the egg for a while longer, perhaps as long as a day and a half. Eventually each egg that has matured enough

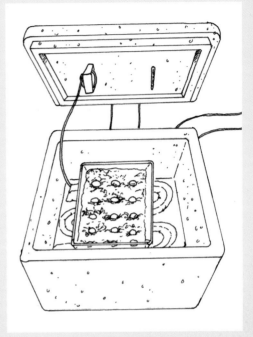

Inside view of incubator, showing thermostat and heat tape. The shoebox holding the eggs rests atop a "rack" of hardware cloth. The incubation medium consists of vermiculite, spagnum moss, or a mixture of peat and soil.

to hatch will. The live babies will emerge from the eggs and can be removed to another terrarium. Although they may not feed immediately, small insects can be offered. A sunning spot may or may not be used. Water should be provided by misting or a drip system.

(If any eggs remain unpipped, continue to incubate them until they go bad.)

When it comes to selecting a chameleon, there's a wide variety to choose from. Some are hardier and more popular than others. Pick the species that you like and that's right for you.

The Veiled Chameleon

An Asocial Arabian Beauty

The veiled chameleon, *Chamaeleo calyptratus*, belongs to the subgenus *Chamaeleo* and comes from the mountainous desert areas of Yemen and Saudi Arabia. It can be found on the western slopes of a mountain range that begins in Yemen and ends in Saudi Arabia, and on the southern slopes of mountains on the tip of Yemen, at the entrance of the Red Sea. Those who keep *C. calyptratus* agree on two things: the species is unique for its beauty and, among the asocial chameleons, this lizard is legendary for its extreme territoriality and aggressive behavior toward its own kind.

Appearance

The specific name refers to the high hood or casque. The casque in the male of the nominate subspecies, measured from the corner of the mouth to the peak, may range from

This female Cameroon mountain chameleon will live well in a cool forest terrarium.

3–4 inches (8–10 cm) in height. This is a truly impressive adornment. The female's casque is much lower.

It appears that the casque has several functions. Among others, it increases the size of the lizard, and so makes it less attractive to potential predators, and it functions as a water condensation site, with the movable occipital flaps channeling the water to the back corners of the mouth. This passive form of water "acquisition" works well in desert areas, where the night-to-day temperature fluctuations result in early morning dew condensation upon cooler surfaces.

Behavior

In the early morning hours, in outdoor caging, as the warming rays of the sun chase the lingering coolness from the easternmost branches of the trees in which these lizards rest overnight, the chameleons stir. They methodically seek out the warmest basking sites amid the branches and turn themselves broadside to the sun. The side facing the sun will darken, increasing the amount of warmth absorbed.

As the lizards warm, they become more active, and they begin to look around. The coloration of the females, which darkens at night, pales to a light green with white or pale yellow spots and vertical streaks. The males also change their coloration. They brighten from their sleeping colors of dull slate or olive yellow to a brilliant series of dark-edged vertical bands of turquoise and bright yellow. The term "gaudy" seems apt. A visible but not particularly prominent vertebral crest is present. The gular crest is more strongly developed, consisting of serrate scales on females and juveniles and of elongate scales on sexually mature males.

The Sexes

The males and females are sexually dimorphic, differing not only in coloration but in size as well. Overall length for the largest males is nearly 2 feet (60 cm), including the tail.

This male veiled chameleon is an example of what hobbyists call the "sunburst phase."

Females are much smaller, attaining a length of about 14 inches (35 cm). Both sexes grow rapidly.

Males have tarsal (heel) spurs; females do not. The function of the spurs is unknown. The spurs are evident even on day-old babies.

Remember that male *calyptratus* are usually aggressive lizards. Some can be unduly aggressive even toward females with whom they are trying to mate. At times this can result in injuries to the female. Watch your lizards until you are certain that all is well. Aggressive behavior is more apt to manifest itself if the lizards are kept in small cages, or, if in large cages, where there are too few visual barriers. Adding visual barriers, no matter the size of the cage, may help stave off some savagery.

We kept a trio of *calyptratus* (one male and two females) together for several years. Their cage measured 4 × 2.5 ×6 feet (120 × 75 × 180 cm) and contained the usual crisscross of branches provided by a potted fig tree. Despite the fact that the male was one of the largest specimens we'd ever seen and that the females were small to average in size, no problematic interactions ever occurred. Both females produced several clutches of eggs throughout the warmer months of each year.

Breeding Behavior

Veiled chameleons, both male and female, signal their breeding receptivity via skin coloration and patterning. For instance, a female *calyptratus,* when relaxed and unthreatened, displays her passive coloration of pale green with rows of white patches and dots. When receptive to breeding, she usually (but not always) adds sky blue "flash" markings along the back and tail and on the casque.

When you wish to breed your chameleons, if your male and female are not kept together as a matter of course, let them see each other for a few minutes (or hours) before you put them together.

If the female is not interested in breeding, her coloration will darken upon sight of the intended male. She will straighten her legs to stand erect, flatten her body, and warn him off with darkened coloration of dark green or black accented with bright blue and yellow spots. She will rock back and forth on her perch, expand her gular area, and fixedly stare at the male. If the male approaches too closely, she will gape her mouth and exhale sharply. If this continues, try another male. Perhaps he will be more acceptable.

The male *calyptratus* reacts to the sight of a female (or another male) with a typical male lizard territorial display. His colors brighten. He laterally flattens his body to appear larger, puffs out his throat area, and nods his head. He approaches the female with a characteristic side-to-side swinging walk (almost a swagger), which helps show off his size and coloration. His tail will be tightly curled. It is at this stage that he is the most aggressive toward the female. He may bite and butt her repeatedly, hard enough to cause permanent damage. If extreme aggression occurs, the two must be separated. Try again later.

If the female is receptive to the advances of the male, she will keep her receptive coloration, turn, and slowly walk away. The male will follow, oftentimes butting her on the hips and tail region with his closed mouth. He will then mount her and juxtapose their vents. He will deposit sperm in her cloaca with one of his two hemipenes and then dismount. The entire mating may take several minutes and can be repeated several times in one day.

The Gravid Female

A female that has been impregnated will begin to reject all males anywhere from 18 hours to 3 days after the copulation. She will demonstrate this rejection by evoking her darkened warning coloration upon sighting another *calyptratus,* male or female. When left alone or unstressed, a gravid female may display her normal passive coloration or her receptive breeding coloration of green and white with blue flashings.

Gravid female *calyptratus* exhibit increased basking time just before egg deposition. Since the sun's UV rays (between the wavelengths of

290 and 315 nanometers) are essential for the conversion of vitamin D_3, it seems that this increased basking time has a very real function.

Even after laying her eggs, the female usually will continue to display warning coloration to any male encountered for several weeks following egg deposition. After that she may display her receptive coloration, although she does not need to mate again to lay her next clutch of fertile eggs.

In captivity *Chamaeleo calyptratus* is a fecund species. Captive females first become receptive to mating for a period of 10 to 15 days at the very young age of 3½–5 months. They are again receptive to mating about 60 days after egg deposition. Captive females that are not bred during that first receptive period almost always die egg-bound when they do become gravid.

The females can lay multiple clutches after a single mating. Females lay clutches of 27 to 80 eggs three to four times a year, with the larger females laying the larger clutches. This sort of deposition seriously depletes the strength of the female. Captive females rarely live beyond their fifth or sixth clutch.

In contrast, *C. calyptratus* in the wild lay far fewer eggs, from 12 to 20. It is not known specifically what regulates the clutch size or accounts for the discrepancy between captive and wild examples. Perhaps seasonal or daily temperature fluctuation, changed nutritional levels, or other unidentified factors are responsible. Neither do we know how long the females live in the wild.

Nest Preparations

Gravid female veiled chameleons look distinctly gravid, with almost half their total weight coming from the eggs. A few days before deposition, a female will stop eating and begin searching the bottom of the cage for a proper egg deposition site. She will explore her cage carefully before choosing a nest site. This is the time to provide a solitary enclosure with a nesting area for the female if she is being kept in a group enclosure.

The female will dig a tunnel for her egg site, using her front paws to dig and shoving the loosened dirt out behind with her hind legs. The tunnel will be wide enough for the lizard to turn around, and long enough so she can turn around and still be hidden within the tunnel. She will dig until the tunnel is about 12 inches (30 cm) deep. The process may take her 18 hours.

She will deposit her eggs at the end of the tunnel and cover them with soil while posi-

An adult male veiled chameleon sits quietly on a limb.

The panther chameleon (shown here) vies with the veiled chameleon for hobbyist popularity.

tioned "nose out," using her front legs to pull the soil into the tunnel and her hind legs to push the soil back down into the tunnel. Once the eggs are covered loosely by the soil, she will emerge and depart. Offer her water and food as soon as she is done because her body reserves have been depleted by the egg formation and the exertion of egg deposition.

When incubated at 78 to 80°F (25–27°C), hatching takes from seven to eight months. Although it is usually reported that all of the eggs in a clutch hatch simultaneously (especially when the eggs are in contact with each other), many of the clutches that we have incubated hatch over a period of 6 to 10 days. Most clutches have had a 100 percent hatch.

Dietary Needs

A diet of well-fed vitamin-dusted crickets, giant mealworms, non-noxious grasshoppers (do not feed lubber grasshoppers to the lizards), waxworms, and assorted greens will keep your *calyptratus* healthy. Please note, you need to feed gut-loaded crickets (see page 35). Unlike most other chameleon species, most veiled chameleons will eat a substantial percentage of finely chopped greens and some grated root vegetables and fruit (collards; romaine; the blossoms of nasturtium, hibiscus, dandelion, and rose; escarole; turnips; carrots; figs; and apples). Vegetation is an important dietary component for this chameleon.

▬▬▬ T I P ▬▬▬

Food Choices

Dietary variation is the key to success. Offer:

✔ crickets
✔ giant mealworms
✔ butterworms
✔ waxworms
✔ field plankton
✔ roaches
✔ pinky mice, if your specimens are particularly large

Some *pardalis* will also accept nontoxic blossoms such as dandelions, nasturtiums, and rose petals.

The second subspecies of the veiled chameleon, *C. c. calcarifer*, has a much lower head casque. They are also somewhat smaller and much less frequently seen as captives.

The Panther Chameleon

Showy, Variable, and Hardy

A denizen of varied habitats, the panther chameleon, *Furcifer pardalis*, can be found along the northwestern, northern, and east coast of mainland Madagascar. It also occurs on many coastal islands. It is found from sea level to elevations of 4,000 feet (1,230 m) and from scrublands to open secondary forest. Temperature within its range varies from the high 90°F (36°C) on summer days to 35°F (2°C) on winter nights.

The panther chameleon is most common in warm, humid climates with a moderate seasonal fluctuation. They do not like deeply shaded forest habitat and are what we would term a "forest-edge" species, preferring areas where the forest borders agricultural habitat.

The species is sexually dimorphic, with the males reaching a total length of 22 inches (56 cm) and the females reaching 13 inches (33 cm). Males have a small, vaguely forked rostral projection.

Male Coloration

The panther chameleon males are known for spectacular color variations among populations. The colors are most intense during breeding season. Most males have varying amounts of red or orange on the face, legs, and tail, but the color variations get wilder from there.

The males from Nosy Be, a small island off the northwestern tip of Madagascar, are uniform light blue-green to turquoise with a light to white side stripe. Their lips are bright yellow. Other males from Nosy Be are uniformly turquoise and are called, with an odd sort of logic, "blue phase." Body bars on these are usually faint or absent.

Males from Ambanja, a coastal town just across the waterway from Nosy Be, are light blue-green with bright burgundy or red vertical body bars, highlighted with the horizontal light stripe on each side. The lips are light colored. During social displays, the eye turrets of these males flush with patterns of red, yellow, or green.

Males from Diego Suarez, at the far northern tip of Madagascar, resemble the males from Ambanja but can change their body color from

This is a very pretty rainbow-hued panther chameleon.

green to yellow (the body bars and eye turrets of burgundy remain).

Males from the eastern coast of Madagascar, from the towns of Maroansetra to Tamatave, are usually dark green with no or only vague body bars. The dorsal crest, the area along the backbone, is usually lighter and forms a gray stripe. The broken stripe along the side of the body is a pale fawn color, while the eye turrets color up during social display to a distinctive pattern of black and gray. Males from at least two of these eastern coastal populations can change their coloration from dark green to a uniform bright orange-red in a matter of seconds. The more brilliantly red specimens are from the towns of Sambava and Maroansetra on the northeastern tip of Madagascar.

Female Coloration

Most females exhibit little change from population to population. Females are usually pale gray-green with vertical russet bands. One notable exception was a female from north-eastern Madagascar that was (and remained) brilliant orange with brown bands. A prominent white lateral stripe was present.

In fact, the presence of a light, longitudinal midlateral stripe on each side is a constant for both sexes.

Courtship Routines

As with other species of chameleons, if the male and female panther chameleon have not been kept together, it is best to let them see each other before placing them in the same enclosure for breeding. After a few minutes, the male will have usually cooled off enough (and the female will have indicated interest, as demonstrated by her coloring) for courtship to proceed.

When the female *pardalis* is interested in breeding, she will exhibit her receptive coloration. Her body coloration will fade to an overall white or fawn, turning to pale pink on her underside. If she is not interested, she will darken in tone, her crossbars more distinctive,

gape her mouth, and turn so her side view is visible to the male.

The male will indicate his interest by the increased brilliance of his body color and eye turret color, much the same changes as in male-to-male encounters, but his behavior will be far less aggressive. The male will bob his head and approach the female.

If the female is receptive, she will keep her pale coloration. The male will mount her and twist so their vents are juxtaposed. Copulation may last from 10 to 30 minutes.

The Gravid Female

Once gravid, the female panther chameleon will display a new color pattern, one of overall earthen tones with a series of orange or tan

Chameleons, like this male Usumbara giant three-horned chameleon, sleep soundly, often contrast with their background, and may then be easily approached.

"portholes" on each side. She will not be receptive to any males while gravid (although she will again become receptive two to three weeks after egg deposition).

The female can produce several egg clutches a year, with 12 to 50 eggs per clutch. Incubation takes from 6 to 12 months and, at least in the wild, appears to be timed so the young emerge during the warm season. Those young that survive until the next warm season are sexually mature and begin breeding. There is a high mortality among egg-laying females, and it appears that few of them survive beyond the second year, either in the wild or in captivity.

The gravid female needs to be isolated and provided with an egg-laying area three to six weeks after breeding. She will dig a tunnel in a container of moistened sand or potting soil, lay her eggs and fill the tunnel with the loosened soil. As soon as she has completed tamping down the dirt in the tunnel, offer her food and water.

When incubated at 73 to 76°F (22–25°C), the eggs (as many as 32) hatch in about five and a half months.

Male *pardalis* are highly territorial during the breeding season. They team up with females only during the breeding season, preferring to remain well-spaced in their habitat of low-growing trees and shrubs. Both sexes seem to prefer to stay 6 feet (1.8 m) or so off the ground, although they occasionally are found higher up.

Male-to-male reactions include a territorial display of lateral body compression, puffing out the gular area, tail coiling, and dramatic color changes of the eye turrets. The male seeking to dominate will move toward his rival. If the rival does not retreat, the challenger will begin the fight, which sometimes starts with a head butting contest and progresses to biting and lunging. If they are not separated, serious injury will occur.

Diet

Panther chameleons have a hearty appetite and eat almost the equivalent of their body mass per week in vitamin-dusted, gut-loaded (VDGL) crickets—this translates to the active consumption of 30 to 50 crickets a week—and other insects. As with other chameleons, pan-thers will tire of a diet that consists of the same type of insects day after day.

Of the many chameleon species available, *F. pardalis* is one of the most desirable from the herpetoculturist's viewpoint. They are beautiful, variable, hardy, and prolific. There could hardly be a better suite of characteristics.

Jackson's, Johnston's, Usumbara Giant, and Poroto Mountain Three-Horned Chameleons

African Horned Chameleons

The Jackson's, Johnston's, Usumbara giant, and Poroto three-horned chameleons (and numerous others) belong to the subgenus *Trioceros*.

The Poroto three-horned, *Chamaeleo fuelleborni*, and the Usumbara giant three-horned, *Chamaeleo demerensis*, are rather poorly known in herpetocultural circles. The former is apparently restricted in distribution to the Ngosi Volcano in Tanzania's Poroto Mountains. The latter is more widely distributed in the Usumbara and Uluguru Mountains of Tanzania. The Poroto three-horned chameleon, an 8½-inch-long (21-cm), rough-skinned forest dweller of moderately high elevations, produces up to 15 live babies in a single litter annually. This species varies from forest green to rich brown in color. Although the Usumbara three-horned chameleon is also thought to have only a single clutch annually, it is an egg-layer that produces from 10 to as many as 60 eggs at each laying. An adult measures about a foot (30 cm) in length. Although not of spectacular coloration, the yellow-highlighted dull green of the content adult is pretty. If stressed, the body becomes profusely dotted with black. Both of these species do best at temperatures that fluctuate between 58°F (15°C) at night and 84°F (28°C) during the day. They are relatively hardy as captives, and if their need for high humidity and cool temperatures is addressed, they do well.

The Johnston's Chameleon

The Johnston's chameleon, *Chamaeleo johnstoni*, hails from moderate elevations in the forests of equatorial central Africa. The two (some authorities feel there are three) subspecies occur in habitats as diverse as savannas and cloud forests. The habitats are damp and well watered and average between 55°F on the coolest nights to nearly 85°F on the warmest days (13-29°C). Although there is not a lot of rain (40 to 65 inches [100-165 cm] annually), neither is there a well-pronounced dry season. The damp warmth allows *C. johnstoni* to be active year-round.

Male *C. j. johnstoni* have three long, annulated horns. The pair of preorbital horns often curve gently downward; the rostral horn may curve very gently upward. Females lack horns. Both sexes of *C. j. ituriensis* (another subspecies of *johnstoni*) lack horns. Healthy, nonstressed male *C. johnstoni* are typically bright and attractive bluish green. Four broad, irregularly edged dark bands are often visible, as are variably placed blue patches and dark flecks. Yellowish areas may occur dorsolaterally in the green areas. Males occasionally exceed a foot (30 cm) in total length. The females are somewhat smaller. Most females measure between 9 and 11 inches (12–28 cm) in total length.

Sexually receptive females are a more or less vaguely patterned (almost unicolor) bluish green. The dark bandings, when present, are most prominent dorsally. The sides of the female's head often bear turquoise and peach markings. Nonreceptive females are much more strongly banded and brightly colored. The peach markings on the face may brighten to a rather brilliant orange. Although two males cannot be kept together, a single male will usually coexist harmoniously with from three to five females.

Johnston's chameleons have from 5 to more than 20 eggs in a clutch. At an incubation temperature of 72 to 76°F (22–25°C), hatching can occur in about three and a half months.

The Jackson's Chameleons

As with other chameleons, the common name actually refers to several subspecies. With the group known as "the Jackson's," there are three subspecies. Two of the three races are rather readily available commercially.

The Meru Mountains Jackson's chameleon, *C. j. merumontana*, is a smaller race and the least common of the three in American herpetoculture. It commands both common and scientific names from the Tanzanian mountain range to which it is endemic. Both males and females have preorbital and rostral processes.

The nominate race, *C. j. jacksonii*, is the more common of the two smaller forms. Males attain a length of about 10 inches (25 cm); females are somewhat smaller. The males are typically triceratops-like in appearance; the females usually have a rostral process (obscure to prominent) but lack the preorbital processes. This race occurs widely in Kenya and Tanzania but is absent from the Arusha district of the

Note the turreted eyes and annulated horns of this adult male Meru Mountain Jackson's chameleon.

Meru Mountains of Tanzania and the southern slopes of Mt. Kenya, Kenya. In the former it is replaced by the beforementioned *C. j. merumontana* and in the latter by the larger and beautiful *C. j. xantholophus*.

When hobbyists mention *Chamaeleo jacksonii* (or simply "Jackson's chameleon") without designating a subspecies, it is usually the beautiful Mt. Kenyan *C. j. xantholophus* about which they are speaking. It is the largest subspecies and the one most frequently available to herpetoculturists.

The males of this form can reach slightly over 13 inches (33 cm) in total length, and the females are only slightly smaller. The females lack both preorbital and rostral processes.

The Mt. Kenyan Jackson's chameleon has been introduced to at least one of the Hawaiian Islands (Maui) and is also known to exist in the vicinity of Morro Bay, California.

Although capable of considerable color changes, the Mt. Kenyan Jackson's chameleon is usually some shade of green. This may vary from almost black if the animals are severely stressed to a basically unpatterned lime green when they are courting. A bright green appears if the males are involved in territorial displays. An overall light green is assumed when sleeping. A rather deep olive with darker banding or irregular flecking is not uncommon when they are content. Deep olive-brown is also a regularly seen color. Complex lichenate colors and patterns are frequently assumed. A thin to thick, light dorsolateral line, either entire or broken into dashes, may or may not be present. In other words, variability is the name of the

Adult female Mt. Kenya Jackson's chameleons are often an intricate pattern of greens.

game with the juveniles and adults of this wonderful lizard. The neonates are most often tan or a very light gray.

Males are very territorial, defending their range (often a single large tree) against other males by display (posturing and color changes), jousting (horn-to-horn combat), or actual biting.

In the United States, the most success with this species in captivity has been achieved in coastal southern California. There they can be kept outdoors year-round. This is a temperature-tolerant species that would prefer daytime highs in the 74 to 84°F (23–28°C) range with drops at night to 50 to 64°F (10–17°C). They can with-stand temperatures much cooler than this (even sustaining freezing temperatures for very short periods) but dislike warmer temperatures.

The 8 to 50 babies (usually 15 to 25) are born enclosed in sticky, membranous sacs. The sacs readily adhere to branches and leaves, but may also be merely dropped to the ground. The neonates tear themselves free from their birth sacs soon (usually within 10 minutes) after

being expelled by the female. If the relative humidity is low, the birth sacs may dry very quickly, and weaker babies may succumb before being able to emerge. Keep nighttime lows above 68°F (20°C) for the first few weeks of their lives. Two clutches may be produced annually by adult females.

Jackson's chameleons are fairly long lived. Under suitable conditions a life span of a decade may be attained.

High-Casqued, Two-Striped, Elliot's, and Uganda Mountain Chameleons

Some Dwarf Mountaineers

As adults, these four small, live-bearing chameleons attain a length of about 6 inches (15 cm). They belong to the subgenus *Trioceros* and are occasionally available in the pet trade. All are live bearing, having one or two litters of

Female high-casqued chameleons are smaller, less colorful, and have smaller casques than the males.

from 2 to 20 babies annually. All are attractive, and some are actually beautiful. Because of their habitat preferences, not all are easily kept in captivity. In fact, the Uganda mountain chameleon, *Chamaeleo rudis*, occurs so high in the mountains that it is considered an alpine species. The two-striped chameleon, *C. bitaeniatus*, occurs to an elevation of 9,000 feet (2,700 m). Providing cage conditions for the remaining two, the high-casqued chameleon (*Chamaeleo hoehnelii*) and Elliot's chameleon (*C. ellioti*), both of lower elevations, is less demanding. These four species are found in eastern Africa, centering primarily in Tanzania, Uganda, Zaire, and Rwanda.

Although the height of the casque varies on *C. hoehnelii*, it is always prominent and is highest on adult males. This is a rough-scaled little chameleon with both a prominent gular crest and a prominently serrate vertebral crest. They

Adult male high-casqued chameleons are aptly named.

are attractively but not brightly colored. The body coloration is usually a combination of greens and tans, and a pair of light stripes is usually readily discernable on each side.

Elliot's mountain chameleon is often of more pallid coloration and has a proportionately lower

casque than *C. hoehnelii*. The two lateral stripes may be tinged with pink or peach. Again, the male is the brightest and has the highest casque.

Of the four, the two-striped chameleon is most likely to have the stripes fragmented by three large, light or dark blotches on each side. Conversely, the stripes may be prominent and divide the side blotches. The ground color varies from brown or tan to lime green. Like all members of this group, the scales are rough, a casque is present, and a serrate vertebral crest is prominent.

The Uganda mountain chameleon may be brown at times and bright green at others. The lateral markings may be in the form of stripes or spots, and are often lemon yellow.

All four of these chameleons require a high relative humidity and relatively cool temperatures (58–60°F night, 75–85°F days [15–16°C, 21–29°C]) to thrive. A hot basking spot of 82 to 88°F (27–31°C) should be provided, especially for gravid females.

Four-horned chameleons (female, opposite page) are a moderately sized species from tropical West Africa.

The Cameroon Mountain and the Four-Horned Chameleons

A Study in Greens

Two west African beauties, the Cameroon mountain and four-horned chameleons, are clad in the prettiest of imaginable greens—the shades of new leaves, over which play gentle hues of blue and peach. Females of both species may be darker than the males and may have broad, white crossbands dorsally. Females that have been introduced to males but are not receptive to breeding often darken to nearly black in overall coloration. In a word, these chameleons are spectacular.

Both the Cameroon mountain, *Chamaeleo montium*, and the four-horned, *C. quadricornis*, belong to the subgenus *Trioceros*.

Some taxonomists feel that besides the nominate forms of each, *C. montium* is represented by three additional forms and *C. quadricornis* by one. For our purposes we will ignore that possibility. Both *C. montium* and *C. quadricornis* are montane chameleons of moderate size, and both are from the country of Cameroon (Cameroun) in west Africa.

The four-horned chameleon was long thought to be a rarity. However, since the late 1980s both this species and *C. montium* have arrived in the United States and Europe in small numbers. Although *C. quadricornis* is said by some authors to be a species of savanna-edge habitats, other authorities claim it to be a species of cool, wet forest habitats.

The mountain chameleon is a species of humid, cool high-altitude forests. It is somewhat darker than the four-horned chameleon and the arrangement of the horns is very different. Male *montium* have only two large horns. Initially, these diverge slightly, then curve and point straight forward for their distal half.

Horns and Crests

On the other hand, the horns of the quite inappropriately named four-horned chameleon are proportionately shorter. This species actually has three pairs of horns on the snout. Of graduated size, the longest pair are anterior-most in the sequence and are directed upward. The posterior pair may be nothing more than an enlargement of single scales on each side of the snout. The middle pair are of intermediate length and are often directed slightly outward. The females of both species have only nubbins (if anything) to represent the horns.

The males of both species have rather low, prominently ribbed vertebral crests, which continue to and proportionately heighten on the basal third of the tail. It is from these crests that both species derive a secondary pet-store name—sailfin chameleon.

The males of both species near a foot (30 cm) in total length; the females are two to three inches (5–7.5 cm) shorter.

Despite coming from a country that lies only a few degrees north of the equator, the mountain and four-horned chameleons occur at elevations that assure that both species are perpetually cool. At the upper end of the seventies (25°C), both begin to show signs of discomfort; if allowed to go above the very low eighties (27°C) both species become acutely distressed. The rainfall in their mountain homes is also considerable, though seasonable, to a degree. There are two pronounced rainy seasons, broken by two poorly defined "dry" seasons. The term "dry" is a comparison only and if taken literally would be a misnomer. The temperatures of these mountain fastnesses range from the high 50s to the very low 80s (14–28°C). As might be surmised, the nearly daily rains assure a very high relative humidity in these mountain forests, and the nearly continual cloud cover prevents all but intermittent sunlight. These are conditions that should be duplicated in the terrarium. Even when provided with a basking lamp, the specimens we have kept have shown little inclination to use it.

When sleeping, both of these chameleons lower their heads to the branch on which they are sitting and coil the tail into a tight watch spring. At this time they are in appearance very much like a broad, pale green leaf.

Although many authors have suggested keeping the sexes separate, I have seen no adverse interactions when they are maintained as pairs or trios. Of the two, *C. montium* seems the more aggressive. Hatchlings can also be kept communally. Until sexual maturity is attained, baby males seem no more aggressive than females. If you do maintain these creatures communally, you must take the time to ascertain that all are getting their share of the food insects. As with many reptiles, there will be some specimens that feed more readily than others.

Reproduction

Both mountain and four-horned chameleons are oviparous. Females have rather small clutches of fairly large eggs (typically 5 to 12, rarely 16). At a temperature of from 70 to 72°F (21–22°C), incubation durations vary from four and a half to just under six months. It is not uncommon for all hatchlings to emerge within a few hours of each other. The hatchlings are about an inch and a half in length and will begin eating termites and pinhead crickets within a few hours of hatching. If amply fed, the growth of the young of both species is rapid. They have been known to reach sexual maturity within a period of seven months.

The Carpet Chameleon

A Mosaic of Diversity

The carpet chameleon, *Furcifer lateralis*, derives its common name from the intricate pattern and brilliant colors of the gravid females, which remind one of the richness of an oriental carpet. This Malagasy species occurs at moderate altitudes where temperatures are also moderate. Both sexes reach a length of 7½ to 10 inches (17–25 cm).

Coloration

Males are green and have a thin, white mid-lateral line. Gravid females have a pattern of brown bands separated by cream or yellow,

The spiny chameleon is one of the largest and least colorful of the Madagascar species.

dark lateral ocelli (open-centered rings), often a poorly defined rich orange or orange-red midlateral stripe, a tan-peppered brown belly, and yellow-peppered brown legs. The throat and lips are spotted and striped, dark on light. The tail is barred for its entire length. Non-gravid females lack the richness of color but are rather similarly marked. Neither sex has facial or crown adornments. This is a short-lived (18 to 36 months), rather delicate chameleon. Gravid females are especially deli-cate and easily stressed, and since almost every female carpet chameleon received in the United States is gravid (as well as dehydrated), it is small wonder that the mortality is high.

This species should be housed in a well-ventilated terrarium having a daytime high of 78 to 84°F (23–28°C) and a nighttime low of 66 to 72°F (18–22°C). Gravid females should not be subjected to temperatures below 70°F (21°C) and should be provided with a hot spot of about 90°F (32°C). Newly received specimens should be checked immediately for endoparasites.

Female carpet chameleons will lay several clutches of from 10 to 20 eggs annually. Incu-bation temperatures of 70 to 75°F (21–24°C) seem best. At the high end of this range, incu-bation will take somewhat less than six months.

Oustalet's Chameleon and the Spiny Chameleon

Two Giant Malagasy Chameleons

Two large species of the genus *Furcifer* are the most generally distributed chameleons on Madagascar. Oustalet's chameleon, *Furcifer*

oustaleti, the world's largest species, is found virtually all over the island. The very similar appearing and only slightly smaller *F. verrucosus*, often called the spiny chameleon, is more restricted in distribution, occurring mainly in the south and western parts of the island. Neither species has rostral adornments, but *F. verrucosus* has enlarged cheek scales and a more spinous vertebral crest.

Oustalet's Chameleon

In the wild, the widespread and adaptable Oustalet's chameleon is often found in pairs. Males of this long and lanky chameleon are usually some shade of brown, tan, or gray, with broad, vertical russet or deep brown bands of varying intensity. Gravid females can actually be somewhat pretty, often assuming a golden hue with dull red bands and spots. Occasional females may have a blush of olive green suffusing their sides. Both a gular and a dorsal

Flap-necked chameleons are pretty, but wild-collected examples are difficult to acclimate.

crest of small spines are present, as is a rather prominent casque. Females are considerably smaller and have a much reduced casque. The cheek scales of this species are small.

Average-sized males are 2 feet (61 cm) in length; large males are 27 to 28 inches (56–71 cm); exceptional males have been measured at more than 30 inches (76 cm); the largest known male measured a shade more than 32 inches (81 cm).

This is a very hardy chameleon that has been captive bred under varying conditions. *Furcifer oustaleti* from high altitudes produce only a single large clutch of eggs annually. The eggs can number more than 40. At a temperature of 74°F (23°C), incubation can last for more than nine months. The low-altitude examples of this species may have two clutches annually. The egg clutches of specimens from lower elevations may also average more in number, occasionally including more than 60 eggs. At 80°F (27°C), these eggs will hatch in about seven months.

The Spiny Chameleon

The spiny chameleon is often found in and along clearing edges and in roadside shrubbery. Males tend to be dark green on the anterior portion of the trunk. A strongly serrate dorsal crest begins on the neck. The crest of the female tapers and ends at mid-body. Both sexes have large scales scattered over the surface of the body. Females are usually darker than the males.

Like Oustalet's chameleon, the spiny chameleon is big and rather slender. Adult males may exceed 22 inches (55 cm) in total length; females are often less than half that length.

Green or gray, with or without darker spots, are the typical colors of healthy Senegal chameleons.

The 10 to 20 eggs hatch after about seven months at a temperature of 72°F (22°C).

Both Oustalet's and the spiny chameleon bask extensively and are capable of brumating for several weeks in the winter.

The Graceful, Flap-Necked, and Senegal Chameleons

A Trio of Common and Delicate Chameleons

Despite being abundant in the wilds of tropical Africa, wild-collected graceful, flap-necked, and Senegal chameleons suffer a tremendous mortality in captivity. Most succumb soon after import to heavy loads of nematodes. These three species are often seen in pet shops, and because they are quite inexpensive, they are often attractive to potential hobbyists.

It is difficult for beginning hobbyists to understand that not all chameleons are equally easy to keep, and that it would be better to

spend $75 for a species that would live rather than $25 for one that often quickly dies.

But with that said, it is necessary to mention that captive-hatched babies of all three species are relatively hardy. Most of these are not produced through captive breeding; they are the result of eggs taken from freshly dead imported chameleons, then hatched.

Males of the graceful, Senegal, and flap-necked chameleons are extremely aggressive, not only to others of their own species, but, because they are so closely allied, to those of the other two species (and to the common chameleon, *C. chamaeleon*) as well. Family groups of one male and three females of the same species, if healthy and housed in large cages, seem compatible.

These three chameleon species, all members of the genus *Chamaeleo*, are of rather similar external appearance. All attain a length of about 12 inches (30 cm).

The flap-necked chameleon's (*C. dilepis*) common name is derived from the proportionately large, medially divided occipital lobes. The lobes are movable and a displaying adult may hold the flaps at almost right angles to the head, an impressive sight. The occipital lobes of

Hatchling Meller's chameleons are clad in bars of dark gray and white.

the Senegal and graceful chameleons are reduced or absent.

The vertebral, gular, and midventral crests of the flap-necked chameleons are quite prominently developed. The light (often white) ventrolateral line is usually well developed on this species. It begins just posterior to the apex of the forelimb and runs diagonally upward to a point above the rear limbs. The light dorsolateral line is only weakly evident at best. Ground color may be green, tan, or brown. Males have a small tarsal protuberance, and the interstitial throat skin is yellow to orange.

In the wild, this is a prolific chameleon species. Annually, large females produce one or two clutches that number from 15 to 60 eggs. The incubation period lasts from nine to ten months at temperatures of from 78° to 83°F (26–28°C). Sexually receptive females assume a pattern of light spots on a green ground color.

The graceful chameleon, *Chamaeleo g. gracilis*, may be brown, yellow, or blue-green with a pale band on each side. The interstitial gular skin of the males is often a brilliant yellow to orange. When displaying males inflate their throats, the brilliant interstitial skin becomes prominently visible. The body hue becomes a much brighter green, and broad vertical bars and spots of dark olive-black or jet black appear. These displays are used in both territorial situations and courtship. The males of one subspecies of the graceful chameleon (*C. g. etiennei*) lack tarsal spurs, which are prominent on males of the nominate race.

At 77 to 80°F (25–27°C) the 22 to 50 eggs of the graceful chameleon will hatch in somewhat more than seven months. The hatchlings seem much hardier and less nervous than the adults.

The Senegal chameleon, *C. senegalensis,* normally varies in color from green to tan to olive, with or without a profusion of dark leopard spots. There appears to be two subspecies, and the males may or may not have tarsal spurs. The casque of this species is very small and low.

The incubation of the 20 to 60 eggs takes about six months at 77°F (25°C). In the wild, Senegal chameleons apparently lay at least two clutches a season.

If you are inclined to try your hand at imported specimens, do everything possible to ease stressful conditions. Initially, keep each chameleon entirely isolated from others; offer easily digested foods, vitamins, and minerals; and be certain that the lizards remain properly hydrated. Be extremely careful to avoid oversupplementation with vitamins. If it finally looks as if you have a chance with them, have a veterinarian do a fecal float to determine the endoparasites present, and treat as necessary. Females that are gravid (as most imported adults

are) are even more delicate and difficult to acclimatize than males. If your female is gravid and should die, remove the eggs immediately, dry them carefully, and incubate as suggested in the chapter on reproduction.

Meller's Giant Chameleon

An African Giant of Unusual Appearance

A 2-foot-long (60-cm) giant, Meller's chameleon, *Chamaeleo melleri*, is one of the truly beautifully colored chameleons.

This magnificent chameleon from Tanzania and Malawi varies greatly in color. They are typically clad in a ground color of medium green to a forest green so dark that it appears almost black. Over this are bands of variable yellow. Irregular (often profuse) spots of black occur on both the yellow and green bands. When sitting quietly, their tails are usually coiled tight like

The Meller's chameleon is a magnificent tropical African giant.

watch springs. The huge occipital lobes are strongly divided, and the forehead slopes gently downward to a bulbous nose that has just the slightest of rostral protuberances.

Although often called the "giant one-horned chameleon," the rostral extension borne by most *C. melleri* is a pretty poor excuse for a "horn." The big lizards also have prominent, serrate dorsal crests. The Meller's chameleon is sparingly but regularly available in the American and European pet trade.

Chamaeleo melleri not only attains a length greater than that of any other African chameleon species, it is also proportionately heavy bodied. Its diet in the wild includes all manner of suitably sized non-noxious insects and probably the nestlings of any small bird or rodent species the lizard happens across. Certainly, captives show a fondness for pinky mice in addition to the usual insects.

Although *C. melleri* is often referred to as a "cool-weather" chameleon, this does not seem to be true. The species is, apparently, most common in and around savanna habitat and is not at all debilitated by temperatures in the

Male Fischer's chameleons have immense rostral appendages and are beautifully colored.

upper eighties to very low nineties (26–34°C). When temperatures drop into the sixties and seventies (17–25°C), Meller's chameleons bask for long periods.

Meller's chameleons are difficult to sex with a great degree of accuracy. Even fully grown males often have rather small and insignificant hemipenial bulges.

In keeping with their large size, Meller's chameleons can lay up to 70 eggs in a clutch. The hatchlings, which emerge after a period of about seven months of incubation at 70 to 80°F (21–27°C), are gray and black banded.

Fischer's Chameleon

A Forest Beauty

Depending on the subspecies, the rostral processes of the various African Fischer's chameleons, *Bradypodion fischeri*, vary from immense to lacking. Depending on the outlook of the taxonomic authority, there are between three and six very variable subspecies.

Collectively, these chameleons are found in tropical Africa. At adulthood, male Fischer's chameleons may be small (12 to 13 inches [30–33 cm] or large (16 to 19 inches [45–49 cm]).

Appearance

Fischer's chameleons are as often as not a dull brown, with or without vertical banding, but at times they may assume a leaf or forest green, again with or without bands.

The presence or lack of horns is not a reliable method of sexing Fischer's chameleons. Both sexes of *B. f. excubitor* lack horns. While the males of the other subspecies usually have horns, they may be large or small. Most females lack horns, but some females of some subspecies have them. The hemipenial bulges of the males are a more reliable method of sexing Fischer's chameleons.

If not debilitated by collecting and transportation trauma, Fischer's chameleons can be fairly hardy captives. In the wild they range from cool, high-elevation forest habitat to lower savanna areas that are considerably warmer. If you decide to work with *B. fischeri*, watch your specimens very carefully until you determine the exact regimen of temperature and humidity necessary for your animals. If they show distress at warm temperatures, lower the temperature in increments of one or two degrees at a time. If they begin looking dry and uncomfortable, increase the relative humidity in your cage by misting. Fischer's chameleons from damp forested habitats probably bask less than others from more open savanna habitats. Experiment with basking temperatures and monitor

the usage of basking areas by your chameleons as well. Record your findings, listing everything about your lizards that you possibly can. Some dealers (especially specialist reptile importers) may be able to provide you with some bits and pieces of collecting data.

The caging for your Fischer's chameleons will need to vary by the number and size of the specimens with which you are working. In a large cage, a single male and three or four females will coexist well. In a smaller cage, a similar group may be entirely incompatible, requiring that each specimen be caged individually.

Suitably sized insects are eagerly accepted by healthy Fischer's chameleons. Remember to dust the food insects with vitamin D_3 and calcium additives.

Breeding

Fischer's chameleons lay one or more clutches of from 10 to 35 (usually 18 to 24) eggs. Like the care given the chameleons themselves, the care necessary to induce proper development of the eggs can (and will) vary. Eggs from high-elevation adults will need to be incubated at cooler temperatures than eggs from lower elevation specimens. If, even after succeeding this far with your adults, you remain unsure of the proper temperatures, err on the side of coolness. Consider 68 to 70°F (19–21°C) the temperature range at which you will most likely be successful. The eggs of low-elevation *B. fischeri* have been successfully incubated at 75°F (24°C). At that temperature, development takes slightly longer than five months. Incubation would probably be as successful, but take longer, at 70°F (21°C).

Because of the complexities involving the systematics of Fischer's chameleons, if you are

intending to breed the species, it would be best to obtain all of your specimens at the same time from the same source. Often (but not always) all (or most) of the specimens imported together will have been collected from the same general location. It is more likely that your specimens will be genetically compatible if this is the case.

Fischer's chameleons are subtly attractive and reasonably hardy. They are a species with which dedicated hobbyists should be able to succeed.

The Leaf Chameleons

What are the leaf chameleons? Although the very word "chameleon" connotes dramatic color changes, neither the little *Brookesia* of Madagascar nor the closely allied *Rhampholeon* of mainland Africa are capable of much color change. Most are clad in scales of brown and/or tan. Some, especially those that frequent mossy

The Kenya leaf chameleon is rough-skinned and snub-nosed.

tree trunks and limbs, also have patches of moss green. Since for the most part these are creatures of the shadows, whether forest floor or mossy trunk, the browns, tans, and mosses afford these chameleons nearly perfect camouflage. The ventral coloration of some species may be brighter than the dorsal colors.

Preferred Habitat

With the single exception of the armored leaf chameleon, all members of both the genera *Brookesia* and *Rhampholeon* favor areas of humid, primary forests, and according to species, they may be either lowland or montane forest dwellers. In contrast, the armored leaf chameleon, *B. perarmata*, favors the dry, rocky ("tsingy," pronounced just as it's spelled) eroded limestone areas of western central Madagascar.

In this habitat of warm temperatures and low humidity, leaf chameleons occur in vegetation amid and surrounding the rocky pinnacles.

Although currently being scrutinized, at present the Madagascan genus *Brookesia* numbers 22 species. The African genus *Rhampholeon* includes about a dozen species.

Dietary Concerns

As with all chameleons, it is best to provide as varied a diet as is possible for the little leaf chameleons. Over the years ours have readily accepted not only the tiny crickets and termites mentioned earlier, but baby mealworms, small sowbugs, fruit flies, and mixed, suitably sized field plankton as well. At times aphid infestations provide an additional source of food. Since these latter insects often tend to accumulate in vast numbers on the soft growing tips of stems, it is an easy chore to snip the twig free and place the entire thing in the leaf chameleon terrarium.

Although I have not crowded them, I have successfully kept them in tanks (enclosures) proportionately smaller than those that I would use for the more active arboreal chameleons. Although I initially kept four or five specimens in each 20-gallon (76-L) tank, I soon decided to double the size of the individual terraria. I did this by removing an end glass from two 20-gallon tanks and abutting them. The juncture can be sealed with tape or silicone aquarium sealant. The stand on which the tanks are placed must be sturdy and long enough to hold the two tanks end to end. The same space can be created by removing a side glass from

Variable, but always of some shade of brown, the Uluguru mountain leaf chameleon is not a particularly aggressive chameleon.

two aquaria and placing them front to back. However we found that it was easier to provide temperature variations for the lizards in the elongated area than in the widened one. Although I have always kept a very shallow dish of water in the terrarium, I have never seen these lizards drink anything except the droplets of mist from the branches and leaves.

All members of both genera are oviparous. The embryos of many are in a rather advanced developmental stage prior to the eggs being laid. Adult female leaf chameleons lay up to several clutches a year that contain from one to five eggs per clutch. Incubation is of rather short duration, hatching occurring in many cases four to nine weeks subsequent to the deposition date. Depending on normal habitat conditions, the incubation temperatures suggested for captives vary from 68 to 74°F (20–23°C). The eggs of the

lowland forms should be incubated at the warmer temperatures.

The tails of all members of this subfamily are, at best, only moderately prehensile.

Let's take a look at a few of these interesting but little-known and little-studied species. Since none have anything but contrived common names, we will use the names most frequently seen on the various price lists.

Malagasy Species

Thiel's Leaf Chameleon

Brookesia thieli is a moderately sized species, attaining a total length of about 2¾ inches (7 cm). A small but well-defined nasal protuberance is present. The dorsolateral projections number 11 on each side. The supraorbital projections are directed anteriorly and are quite sharp.

Horned Leaf Chameleon

The supraorbital projections of the horned leaf chameleon, *B. superciliaris*, (also mentioned earlier) are somewhat more erect and rather gently rounded. This is a big species, attaining an adult size of nearly 4 inches (10 cm). They have a rather well-defined vertebral ridge and are rather uniformly colored in some shade of brown.

Besides being long, the horned leaf chameleon is rather deep bodied and "hefty" for its length.

Both of the above are species of moderate elevations of eastern Madagascar. When cool nighttime (60 to 65°F [16–18°C]) and daytime (70 to 78°F [21–26°C]) temperatures are provided, these both seem to be hardy chameleon species.

Pygmy Leaf Chameleons

The tiniest of all chameleons are members of the Malagasy *B. minima* complex. Once considered a single species, it is now known that this complex actually consists of at least five very similar and very tiny species. Females, the larger sex, attain a total length of about 1⅜ inches (3.5 cm). The adult males are typically a quarter of an inch smaller, or about 3 cm. Hatchlings are about five-eighths of an inch (1.5 cm) in total length.

Males typically position themselves on the back of sexually receptive females and are carried about for a day or more.

The *minima* group seems to be entirely terrestrial in habit. Although they are not difficult to keep, their minuscule size precludes them accepting all but the tiniest of food insects. The *B. minima* complex of leaf chameleons is restricted to the northern third of Madagascar.

Armored Leaf Chameleon

Although other leaf chameleons are spiny and "of strange appearance," none even come close to equaling the amazing *B. perarmata*. *B. perarmata* imparts none of the feeling of delicacy shown by its congenerics. Instead, it is coarsely scaled, spiny, and tuberculate, and initially reminds an observer more of Australia's thorny devil or America's horned lizards than a chameleon. In short—it is wonderful!

In color, the armored leaf chameleon is brown of body, limb, and tail with a tan to terra-cotta colored head. The dorsal ridges of the posteriorly directed supraocular crests are serrate. Large for a leaf chameleon, *B. perarmata* attains a full 4½ inches (11 cm) in total length.

To date, herpetoculturists have not had much luck keeping the armored leaf chameleon

The horned leaf chameleon is now the most often seen of the Madagascar species.

in captivity. It is possible, since it occurs in a habitat so markedly different from its con-generics, that its diet is different as well. Molochs and horned lizards are ant specialists. Could it be possible that *B. perarmata* is also essentially myrmecophagous?

African Species

The various species of *Rhampholeon* are so similar in appearance that it is best to depend on your supplier for exact identification. Several species are now being regularly imported. Among these are Kersten's leaf chameleon (*R. kersteni*), Uluguru leaf chameleon (*R. ulugurensis*), Nichesi Mountain leaf chameleon (*R. nichisiensis*), stump-tailed leaf chameleon (*B. brevicaudatus*), striped leaf chameleon (*R. spectrum*), and the little *R. temporalis*, a species not yet having an accepted common name.

Most of these species are spinose little lizards that near 3½ inches (9 cm) in length. Like others of the group, they are subtly colored in earthen tones, often russet or terra-cotta on brown or reddish brown. Lateral and dorsal striping may be present (but is often only weakly so). The supraocular crests are anteriorly directed, and tiny rostral processes may be present.

These chameleons are primarily terrestrial but can climb, at least haltingly. All feed readily on tiny crickets, aphids, and termites and avidly on fruit flies and small houseflies.

GLOSSARY

*Here's a list of some of the terms
(along with their definitions)
that appear in this book.
They are applicable to all
reptiles in general.*

Aestivation: a period of warm-weather inactivity, often triggered by excessive heat or drought

Ambient temperature: the temperature of the surrounding environment

Anterior: toward the front

Anus: the external opening of the cloaca; the vent

Arboreal: tree-dwelling

Axillary: near the apex (pit) of the arm

Bicuspid: as used here, pertaining to claws with two points

Brumation: the reptilian and amphibian equivalent of mammalian hibernation

Casque: the upward projecting cap or helmet at the back of a chameleon's head

Caudal: pertaining to the tail

Chromatophore: a pigment-containing skin cell

Cloaca: the common chamber into which digestive, urinary, and reproductive systems

*As with most chameleons, Natal-Midlands
chameleons are brightest when reproductively
active.*

empty and which itself opens exteriorly through the vent or anus

Con...: as used here, a prefix to several words (generic, specific) indicating "the same"; congeneric refers to species in the same genus, conspecific indicates the same species

Cryptic: camouflaged

Deposition: as used here, the laying of the eggs

Deposition site: the spot chosen by the female to lay her eggs

Dermal: relating to the skin

Diapause: a temporary cessation of embryo development, often induced by coolness or dryness

Dichromatic: two color phases of the same species; often sex-linked

Dimorphic: a difference in form, build, or coloration involving the same species; often sex-linked

Diurnal: active in the daytime

Dorsal: pertaining to the back; upper surface

Dorsolateral: pertaining to the upper sides

Dorsum: the upper surface

Endemic: confined to a specific region

Femur: the part of the leg between hip and knee

Flanks: lower side

Form: an identifiable species or subspecies

Fracture planes: softer areas in the tail vertebrae that allow the tail to break easily if seized

Genus: a taxonomic classification of a group of species having similar characteristics; falls between the next higher designation of "family" and the next lower designation of "species"; always capitalized when written (plural: genera)

Glossohyal: a muscle of the extensible tongue.

Granular: pertaining to small, flat scales

Gravid: the reptilian equivalent of mammalian pregnancy

Gular: pertaining to the throat

Although now very expensive and no longer common in the trade, the Parson's chameleon is large, bulky, hardy, and beautiful.

Gular crest: a longitudinal ridge of enlarged throat scales

Heliothermic: pertaining to a species that basks in the sun to thermoregulate

Hemipenes: the dual copulatory organs of male lizards and snakes

Hemipenis: the singular form of hemipenes

Heterogenous: not uniformly sized, colored, or patterned

Homogenous: uniformly sized, colored, or patterned

Horns: as used here, referring to the tapered, rigid, often annulated, forward projecting preocular or rostral processes of chameleons

Hybrid: offspring resulting from the breeding of two species

Hydrate: to restore body moisture by drinking or absorption

Insular: as used here, island-dwelling

Intergrade: offspring resulting from the breeding of two subspecies

Juvenile: a young or immature specimen

Keel: a ridge (along the center of a scale)

Keratin: the hardened, largely inert, protenaceous outer skin of a reptile

Labial: pertaining to the lips

Lateral: pertaining to the side

Malagasy Republic: Madagascar

Melanism: a profusion of black pigment

Mid-dorsal: pertaining to the middle of the back

Midventral: pertaining to the center of the belly or abdomen

Monotypic: containing but one type

Myrmecophagous: eating ants

Occipital lobe: the flaps or lobes of skin at the rear of some chameleons' heads

Ocelli: light, centered rings

Ontogenetic changes: changes occurring during growth

Ontogeny: the course of development

Oviparous: reproducing by means of eggs that hatch after laying

Ovoviviparous: bearing live young in placental sacs

Parietal eye: a sensory organ present in certain reptiles that is positioned midcranially

Phalanges: the bones of the toes

Poikilothermic: a species with no internal body temperature regulation; the old term was "cold-blooded"

Posterior: toward the rear

Preocular: anterior to the eye

Prehensile: grasping

Race: a subspecies

Rostral: pertaining to the nose area

Rugose: not smooth; wrinkled or tuberculate

Serrate: saw-like

Species: a group of similar creatures that produce viable young when breeding; falls beneath genus and above subspecies

Subspecies: the subdivision of a species; a race that may differ slightly in color, size, scalation, or other criteria

Sympatric: occurring together

Tarsal spur: an outgrowth on the heel

Taxonomy: the science of classification of plants and animals

Terrestrial: land-dwelling

Thermoregulate: to regulate (body) temperature by choosing a warmer or cooler environment

Tubercles: warty protuberances

Tuberculate: pertaining to tubercles

Tympanum: the external eardrum

Vent: the external opening of the cloaca; the anus

Venter: the underside of a creature; the belly

Ventral: pertaining to the undersurface or belly

Ventrolateral: pertaining to the sides of the venter

Vertebral: pertaining to the mid-dorsal area

Vertebral crest: a ridge of scales or an actual longitudinal mid-dorsal crest

Note: Other scientific definitions are contained in the following two volumes:

Peters, James A. *Dictionary of Herpetology.* New York: Hafner Publishing, 1964.

Wareham, David C. *The Reptile and Amphibian Keeper's Dictionary.* London: Blandford, 1993.

INFORMATION

There are herpetological clubs based in many larger cities. Pet stores, museums, nature centers, and biology teachers/professors are often able to advise you of the nearest interest group.

E-addresses

A great deal of information is available on the Internet. Using a search engine to review the data for a particular chameleon species will often provide a wealth of information.

Many chameleons, both common and rare, are available at *www.firstchoicereptiles.com* and at *www.gherp.com.*

Reptile and amphibian expos are held throughout America and Europe. One of the largest is the National Captive Breeders Expo (*www.reptilebreedersexpo.com*) in Daytona Beach, Florida.

The Chameleon Journals (*www. chameleonjournals.com*) is an excellent source of online information.

Another information source is The Chameleon Information Network (CiN) (*www.animalarkshelter.org/cin/*).

Accessing *www.arav.org* (Association of Reptilian and Amphibian Veterinarians) will help you locate a veterinarian qualified in reptile medicine.

Newsletters

The International Chameleon Working Group publishes between two and four newsletters annually. c/o Lynn Raw, P. O. Box 200, Merrivale, 3291 South Africa

Additional Reading

Bartlett, Richard. *Properly Caring for True Chameleons.* Mission Viejo, California; *Reptiles Magazine* 1:1; pages 26–33, 1993.
_____ and Patricia Bartlett. *Jackson's and Veiled Chameleons.* Hauppauge, New York: Barron's Educational Series, Inc., 2001.
Branch, Bill. *A Field Guide to the Snakes and Other Reptiles of Southern Africa.* Sanibel, Florida: Ralph Curtis Publishing, 1988.

Werner's chameleons, like this male, are comparative newcomers in the pet trade.

Whether referred to as cute or bizarre, the fringed leaf chameleon, a dweller of the razor-sharp tsingy rock formations in Madagascar, is a delicate and difficult captive.

Cowden, Jeanne. *Chameleons, The Little Lions of the Reptile World*. New York: David McKay, 1977.

De Vosjoli, Philippe, and Gary Ferguson. *Care and Breeding of Panther, Jackson's, Veiled, and Parson's Chameleons*. Santee, California: Advanced Vivarium Systems, 1995.

Glaw, Frank, and Miguel Vences. *A Field Guide to the Amphibians and Reptiles of Madagascar*. Bonn: Privately published, 1994.

Langerwerf, Bert, and Mark Paris. *Super Mealworms*. Mission Viejo, California: *Reptiles Magazine* 2:1; pages 42–46, 1993.

LeBerre, Francois. *The Chameleon Reference Book*. Hauppauge, New York: Barron's Educational Series, Inc., 1995.

Martin, James. *Masters of Disguise, A Natural History of Chameleons*. New York: Facts on File, 1992.

McKeown, Sean. *Hawaiian Reptiles and Amphibians*. Honolulu: Oriental Publishing, 1978.

Preston-Mafham, Ken. *Madagascar, A Natural History*. New York: Facts on File, 1991.

Schnieper, Claudia. *Chameleons*. Minneapolis: Carolrhoda Books, 1989.

The Uganda mountain chameleon is a small Alpine species. When content, females are rather uniformly green. Males, however, often display a broad stripe of yellow on each side.

Numbers in **boldface** type indicate color photos.

Acknowledgments

Many thanks to Nick Mole of First Choice Reptiles (*www.firstchoicereptiles.com*) who provided us opportunity to photograph many of the African chameleon species that are now in the pet trade as well as for information on leaf chameleons. Gary Nafis, Bill Love, and Rob MacInnes of Glades Herp, Inc. (*www.gherp.com*) provided additional information and/or photo opportunities.

Our appreciation is also extended to Bert and Hester Langerwerf, Ken Kalisch, Susan James, Kenn Mease, and the late Sean McKeown.

Our editor, Pat Hunter, smilingly accepted the task of supervising all aspects of our book while Kara Lashley, copy editor, united our split infinitives and propped up our dangling participles. Thank you both.

About the Authors

R. D. Bartlett is a herpetologist who has authored more than 600 articles and numerous books on reptiles and amphibians. He lectures extensively and has participated in field studies across North and Latin America. In 1970 he began the Reptilian Breeding and Research Institute, a private facility. Since its inception, more than 200 species of reptiles and amphibians have been bred there, some for the first time in the United States under captive conditions.

Patricia Bartlett has authored five books on natural history and historical subjects. She has served as editor for an outdoors book publishing firm in St. Petersburg, Florida, has worked for a science museum in Springfield, Massachusetts, and was director of an historical museum in Ft. Myers, Florida.

Important Note

Chameleons may transmit certain infections to humans. Always wash your hands carefully after handling your specimens. Always supervise children who wish to observe your chameleons, and see your physician immediately if you are bitten or scratched.

Photo Credits

All photos © copyright R. D. Bartlett.

Cover Photos

Front, back, inside front, and inside back © copyright R. D. Bartlett.

© Copyright 2005, 1995 by Barron's Educational Series, Inc.

All rights reserved.
No part of this book may be reproduced in any form, by photostat, microfilm, xerography, or any other means, or incorporated into any information retrieval system, electronic or mechanical, without the written permission of the copyright owner.

All inquiries should be addressed to:
Barron's Educational Series, Inc.
250 Wireless Boulevard
Hauppauge, NY 11788
www.barronseduc.com

International Standard Book No. 0-7641-2863-9

Library of Congress Catalog Card No. 2004057354

Library of Congress Cataloging-in-Publication Data
Bartlett, Richard D., 1938–
    Chameleons, a complete pet owner's manual :
    facts & advice on care and breeding /
    R. D. Bartlett and Patricia P. Bartlett.
        p. cm.
    Includes index.
    ISBN 0-7641-2863-9
    1. Chameleons as pets. 2. Chameleons.
    I. Bartlett, Patricia Pope, 1949– II. Title.

SF459.C45B369 2005
639.3'956—dc22   2004057354

Printed in China
9 8 7 6 5 4 3 2 1